MW00365918

BARRELS
&
DRAMS

BARRELS
&
DRAMS

THE HISTORY OF WHISK(E)Y
IN JIGGERS AND SHOTS

edited by William M. Dowd

STERLING EPICURE
New York

STERLING EPICURE
New York

An Imprint of Sterling Publishing
387 Park Avenue South
New York, NY 10016

© 2011 by William M. Dowd
Illustrations © 2011 by Laura Hartman Maestro

A full list of credits for the individual readings appears on pages 217–219.
A full list of picture credits appears on page 220.

ISBN 978-1-4027-7865-0

Library of Congress Cataloging-in-Publication Data

Barrels and drams : the history of whisk(e)y in jiggers and shots / edited by William M. Dowd.
    p. cm.
ISBN 978-1-4027-7865-0
1. Whiskey. 2. Whiskey industry. I. Dowd, William M.
TP605.B37 2011
641.2'52--dc22
                                                                  2010048590

Distributed in Canada by Sterling Publishing
c/o Canadian Manda Group, 165 Dufferin Street
Toronto, Ontario, Canada M6K 3H6

For information about custom editions, special sales, premium and corporate purchases, please contact
Sterling Special Sales Department at 800-805-5489 or specialsales@sterlingpublishing.com.

Manufactured in China

2 4 6 8 10 9 7 5 3 1

www.sterlingpublishing.com

~ CONTENTS ~

NOTE
— *from the* —
AUTHOR

Where, oh where, to begin? And, perhaps just as important a question, where to end?

In telling the story of a phenomenon whose every atom, every nuance, is widely debated in heated arguments and calm discussions often fueled by the very substance itself, there certainly is a starting point. Luckily, there is no end in sight.

So, for the purposes of following the history of whiskey, this tome begins with an overview, then proceeds with essays—about people, places, and processes that have made whiskey such a ubiquitous part of our world—by individuals whose reputations for sound scholarship and enthusiasm for their subject make them boon companions on the printed page or the proverbial pub.

Of course, we cannot begin without a nod to the current mantra in the commercial world of alcoholic beverages, "Drink Responsibly," created by the industry as a response to the effects of binge drinking, the low-quality and sometimes dangerous products in third-world economies, and the rise in alcohol-related accidents.

In truth, though, that has been a plea for generations upon generations. There are even those who think Washington Irving's "Rip Van Winkle," the tale of an early Dutch settler sleeping away twenty years of his life after drinking too deeply from a keg of liquor, is more of a cautionary tale about the evils of alcohol than it is a metaphor for the awakening of a developing America as it has long been labeled.

With all that in mind, let the journey begin.

William M. Dowd
Troy, New York

IN THE BEGINNING

no. 1

"The light music of whiskey falling into a glass—an agreeable interlude."

–Irish novelist James Joyce

AN OVERVIEW
— *of the* —
SPIRITS WORLD

I t is one of the great ironies of our time that the region of the world that gave us the distillation process today is largely off-limits to whiskies and other spirits.

Most cultures have a long relationship with fermented beverages, from the viscous beers of the Egyptian pharaonic era to the milky *pulque* of the Meso-American era in Mexico and Central America. But, that began to change in ancient Mesopotamia (today's Iraq, Syria, and parts of Iran and Turkey) with the development of a rudimentary distillation process usually credited to the brilliant Persian chemist Jabir ibn Hayyan, best known in the Western world as Geber (born CE. 721, died c. 815).

Various liquids were put through the distillation process to become perfumes and medicines, and eventually several beverages of sorts. It was other Arab scientists who advanced the process to the point it was regularly used to make potent beverages, mostly from distilled wine. Now, of course, under the overwhelmingly Muslim constraints of nations that have developed since then in what is widely known as the "cradle of civilization," alcohol is largely prohibited.

Yet, what also remains from Persia beyond the process is the vocabulary of spirits. Take just these two words, for example:

- Alcohol, from *al-koh'l*, the Arabic word for a purified antimony powder used as a cosmetic but which became used by alchemists to refer to any highly purified liquid: that is, distilled wine is the "alcohol" of wine.

- Alembic, a popular type of still, from the Arabic *al-ambiq*, which describes the shape of the vessel.

". . . the word 'whiskey'—spelled with an 'e' in the United States and Ireland or without the 'e' in Scotland, Canada, Japan, India, and elsewhere . . ."

Once the distillation process—essentially the heating of a fermented liquid to turn it to vapor, thus removing many unwanted elements, then allowing it to cool and return to liquid in a more refined form—became commonly known, there were few liquids that escaped being run through it to find acceptable results for human consumption.

In a nod to the ecumenical nature of the spirit, the word "whiskey"—spelled with an "e" in the United States and Ireland or without the "e" in Scotland, Canada, Japan, India, and elsewhere—comes down to us not from Persia, but from the Gaelic word *uisge beatha*—pronounced *wiz key bay tah*—meaning "water of life." (You will see both spellings used throughout this book, depending on the ethnic context.)

That certainly shows whiskey's revered status, either with tongue firmly planted in cheek or as an explanation of a stark reality—that local water throughout much of civilization was unfit for drinking, but nevertheless could be used with a grain mash to create something not only fit for consumption but desired in many forms.

The Lawgivers and the People

"The Glenlivet region, a valley in the Speyside area, is beautiful in spring and summer, but an unforgiving swath in winter months with its craggy peaks, sharply slanted hillsides, and dips and rills . . ."

In the wooded hills above the Glenlivet complex in the Scottish Highlands, I was treated to a view of history and modernity blending as smoothly as the whisky produced by Scotland's oldest licensed distillery.

On two marked trails, one used by the iconic distiller George Smith and one by his contemporaries who smuggled illicit whisky in the eighteenth and nineteenth centuries, I gained a sense of the laborious work and persistence that has always gone into the making and distributing of the storied spirits of Scotland.

From enduring onerous taxes levied by their own government and then by the British Crown to battles over operating illegal stills to internecine battles between rival smugglers and distillers has come today's major industry that is second only to North Sea oil drilling as far as Scotland's revenue is concerned.

The Glenlivet region, a valley in the Speyside area, is beautiful in spring and summer, but an unforgiving swath in winter months with its craggy peaks, sharply slanted hillsides, and dips and rills that allow brisk winds to whip through the glens like sword slashes of icy air.

The region has for centuries produced not only hearty folk but a steady stream of non-peated whiskies—single malts and blends without that signature smoky taste so prevalent in spirits made in other regions of the country. At its height, in the mid- to late 1800s, as many as two hundred small distilleries were operating in the small glen.

The name George Smith is revered there, as the man who refined his whisky so well that it became the favorite of King George IV of Great Britain and, thus, the first Scotch whisky with cachet beyond its immediate environs.

Nearly four thousand miles away in the New World, there is another historic trail—the American Whiskey Trail, which includes seven historic sites and six operating whiskey distilleries spread over a five-state arc between New York and Tennessee by way of Pennsylvania, Virginia, and Kentucky.

If that seems a slightly awkward physical construct, perhaps it is. But it shows the erratic progression of whiskey-making throughout America history, the watershed moment of which occurred before George Smith's rise to prominence.

Traveling from the north, the American Whiskey Trail begins at historic Fraunces Tavern Museum in Manhattan. It was the site of General George Washington's farewell address to his troops in 1783 and operates as a commercial business to this day. The trail ends at the recently rebuilt site of the George Washington Distillery Museum on the grounds of private citizen Washington's home and farm at Mount Vernon, Virginia. There they refer to that site as the gateway to the trail. Geographic chauvinism obviously is dictated by where you live.

In between, visitors take in a string of historic taverns, whiskey museums, and distillery centers. One of them is in the West Overton Museums complex in Scottdale, Pennsylvania, a former distillery center and part of what is billed as the only pre–Civil War village in Pennsylvania still intact. Its heritage links the Old World and the New.

"Among the first Europeans to practice their whiskey-making skills in the United States were the Scots-Irish farmers ..."

Among the first Europeans to practice their whiskey-making skills in the United States were the Scots-Irish farmers who had settled in western Pennsylvania after emigrating from their tempestuous homeland in what now is known as Northern Ireland.

They were not alone in distilling whiskey, but they were among the feistiest and most productive in the New World. That was a legacy of their history of being pushed by the British Crown to populate Northern Ireland because they were Presbyterians who might temper the antipathy of the native Irish Catholics who continually opposed royal rule. However, when you rely too heavily on an intrinsically self-sufficient people, you sometimes don't get the pliable subjects you want. Britain found that to be the case and so raised no particular bar to the stream of Scots-Irish eventually leaving for the United States.

They quickly pushed their way to the frontier area of western Pennsylvania where they found fertile fields for their grain and plenty of takers for the whiskey they produced from some of it. However, when the Continental Congress put a tax on whiskey production—the fledgling nation's first excise tax—they refused to pay, thus touching off the Whiskey Rebellion of 1791 to 1794.

The dispute was about more than simply being taxed. In the minds of a significant number of frontier settlers in the new United States, the government was under control of the eastern elite, and the tax, suggested by Alexander Hamilton, first Secretary of the Treasury, to service the national debt created by the War of Independence, was a prime example of unfairness.

The Whiskey Act of 1791 called for either payment of a flat fee or paying by the gallon. That favored large distillers, most of them operating in the east, because they produced whiskey in volume and could afford the flat fee. Frontier farmers, who generally were small-volume, part-time distillers, wound up paying a higher per-gallon tax, sometimes 50 percent more than the large producers paid.

So acrimonious did the dispute grow that in July 1794, more than five hundred armed Pennsylvanians attacked the home of General John Neville, a federal tax collector. The insurrection quickly was quelled, but the Washington administration knew it had to defuse any further unrest.

Washington and Thomas Jefferson, the latter by then governor of Virginia, cooked up a deal to break up the concentration of resistance. Jefferson offered sixty acres of land as an incentive for moving to the Kentucky region (then part of Virginia), building a permanent structure, and growing corn.

Many of the unhappy Pennsylvanians took advantage of the offer; but they soon realized no family could eat sixty acres' worth of corn a year, and the grain was too perishable to ship out for sale. The Scots-Irish instead hit on the idea of using it to make whiskey in place of much of the wheat and rye they were used to employing. Coincidentally, the presence of massive limestone formations filtered and "sweetened" the water, which helped make a smoother distilled spirit, the one that came to be called bourbon after the Kentucky county in which it was first produced.

(The legal definition of whiskey is a liquor produced from the fermented mash of grains such as barley, corn, and rye and then distilled. Bourbon, however, is a special case. All bourbons are whiskies, but not all whiskies are bourbons. The legal definition of bourbon was codified in 1964 by a U.S. Congressional Resolution requiring that it be a minimum of two years old, at least 80 proof, or 40 percent alcohol by volume [ABV], made from a mash containing at least 51 percent corn, and aged in charred new American oak barrels; the wood and the carbon give it that golden brown color and some of its flavor and aroma.)

Some twenty-five years after the Whiskey Rebellion in America, the unrest in Scotland finally was coming to a close. The unrest there was equal to or more frenzied—and unquestionably longer—than the American ordeal. And, just as was the case in America, it was fueled in large part by a government act.

The Internal Act of Excyse of January 31, 1644, passed by the Scottish Parliament, imposed the country's first duty on spirits; in the vernacular of the day, on "everie pynt of aquavytie or strong watteris sold within the countrey."

Just as in America, the small farmers who were distillers only part-time rose up against this burden that they felt would deprive them of a cost-effective way of using up their excess barley by making a product that could be sold or used for barter.

As was the case in Pennsylvania, the federal government was viewed as a distant, elite group out of touch with the rural farmer/distillers. Luckily for the public good, the Scottish Parliament did little to enforce its new tax for the next half-century or so, but it had planted a seed of distrust.

That distrust remained right through the Act of Union in 1707 when the parliaments of Scotland and England became one. One of the results of that decision was that some of the taxes that had been levied in England, such as the Malt Tax, were spread to the Scots. Food shortages in Scotland caused by poor harvests made the tax all the harder to endure. The activity in smuggling illicit whisky soared.

"... the presence of massive limestone formations filtered and 'sweetened' the water, which helped make a smoother distilled spirit ..."

Over the ensuing years, a string of taxes and regulatory changes were aimed at the whisky industry, a perfect cash cow when it came to raising money for the British Empire's military forces who were regularly engaged in one campaign or another around the globe.

Arguably the most inflammatory was the Walsh Act of 1784 that, though some in Parliament thought it might calm Scottish unrest, was aimed at appeasing the influential Highland distillers who were the most active of the smugglers. It sought to tax only the fermented wash of the process, instead of the finished whisky, and provided that twenty-gallon pot stills, the region's most common, could be made legal upon payment of £1 a year per cubic gallon of capacity. The intent was to retain a tax revenue flow while convincing smugglers that paying the tax could be affordable. In addition, penalties for illegal distilling were increased.

The Walsh Act was a colossal failure. Smugglers did not trust the government, and landowners and merchants who had been benefitting from smugglers who had money to pay their bills didn't want the illicit traffic to stop.

> " Landowners were tired of being forced to pay the fines for smugglers caught plying their trade on leased lands."

Flash forward to about 1820. The tide was turning against the smugglers. Landowners were tired of being forced to pay the fines for smugglers caught plying their trade on leased lands. The government increasingly needed tax revenue and, to keep raising it, passed the Illicit Distillation (Scotland) Act, which elevated penalties to £200 for being in possession of illegal whisky and £100 for owning an unlicensed pot still. The rates were astronomical for the time. The Acts of 1822 and 1823 further enfeebled smuggling in the Highlands by lowering duties on whisky and on licenses and allowing a minimum pot still size of forty gallons.

Although later legislation and meandering public opinion kept the way from being smooth, legal whisky began to become the norm even as foreign markets began to be opened to Scottish spirits.

At one time, most distillers in the Glenlivet, Banffshire, region of Scotland appended the name "Glenlivet" to their products. But, after King George IV (1762–1830) became smitten with George Smith's particular spirit and asked for some of what he termed "THE" Glenlivet whisky during a visit to the region in 1822, eventually the competition was forced to drop the appellation, and Smith co-opted "The Glenlivet" as his own brand name.

To this day, even though the distillery moved to a larger facility just five hundred yards or so away at one time, the same water source—known as Josie's Well—and Scottish barley are used in the double-distilled process.

The Spirit of the Common Man

Scotch whisky, Irish whiskey, American bourbon and rye, Canadian blends, Tennessee whiskey, Japanese single malts . . . the formal names with their highly codified rules of manufacture dominate the world generally classified as "whiskey." To some people, however, rye is rye, Scotch is Scotch, bourbon is bourbon and whiskey is something blended. They make distinctions.

Witness singer-songwriter Don McLean's usage in his [1971] anthemic song "American Pie":

> *"Them good ol' boys*
> *were drinkin' whiskey*
> *and rye . . . "*

Pappy Van Winkle's

family Reserve
Kentucky Straight Bourbon Whiskey
20 years old
750 ml. • Alc. 45.2%/Vol. (90.4 proof)

04.6094 Bottled by Old Rip Van Winkle Distillery • Frankfort, Kentucky

Or, author Mary Chase in her Pulitzer Prize–winning 1944 play *Harvey* in which her central character, Elwood P. Dowd, says:

"I'd just helped Ed Hickey into a taxi. Ed had been mixing his whiskey with his rye, and I felt he needed conveying."

Around the globe, some form or other of homemade, generally unregulated and untaxed—and therefore illegal—whisky or whisky substitute is made from many base ingredients and goes under many names.

In the United States it's old-fashioned moonshine from corn. In Ireland it's *poitin*, or *poteen*, from grain or potatoes. *Langkau* from rice in Malaysia. *Raki* or *rakia* from plums or grapes in Turkey, Greece, Macedonia, and the Serbo-Croatian region. *Filuferru* from grapes on Sardinia. *Siddiq* from sugar water in Saudi Arabia. *Mampoer* from peaches or marula fruit in South Africa. *Boukha* from figs in Tunisia. *Screech* from molasses leftovers in Canada. . . . You get the idea.

No matter the material used, the basic distilling process remains generally the same: create a mash with yeast and grain or other organic matter, let it ferment, then heat the fermented material to turn much of it into steam while the poorer parts separate from it, cool the steam

TASMANIAN
Single Malt Whisky
Small Cask Aged

SINGLE CASK

*L*ARK

43% Alc/Vol   700 mL

PRODUCT OF AUSTRALIA
Produced and bottled by: Lark Distillery Hobart, Tasmania Australia
14 Davey St. Hobart, 7000 TAS
www.larkdistillery.com.au

STANDARD DRINKS 25

This bottle is not chill filtered and as such may develop a slight haze which is natural, characteristic of premium whiskies. Chill filtering removes some of the desirable characters in the whisky. The haze has no effect on the quality of the product.

Small Cask Aged, Single Cask, Single Malt from Tasmania

A note on Barrels and Age Statements

Lark Whisky is matured in barrels specially selected by our distiller. Originally used in the ageing of fine premium Australian Port and Sherry, these casks are coopered into our signature 100L 'Quarter' Cask Barrels. This superior barrel surface offers a more premium wood and is far more active and terms summers encourage a unique dynamic ageing, where the whisky spirit is encouraged to breathe in and out of the oak. These select 'small' cask characters develop rich and complex whisky in less time than commonly possible. Our trophy rubbed, filled with many of the world's most coveted awards is a confirmation enough for us —

BOTTLED

CASK NO

BARREL NO

BREWERY

so it returns to liquid in a purer form, then filter. The process can be repeated several times to continually refine the liquid.

The more popular spirits are aged in wooden casks, but there remains a large market for unaged white spirits in many countries.

The most popular early whiskies were based on rye or barley, those simplest of grains, or a mix of them. In the Western world in particular, the words "rye" and "whisky" were, for generations, virtually synonymous— American rye whiskey, Scottish malt whisky, Irish whiskey, and their ilk made from a rye- or barley-centric mash. The introduction of corn into the mix in the United States resulted in bourbon. And a charcoal filtration method known as the "Lincoln County Process" turned bourbon into an entirely new category, Tennessee sipping whiskey.

Back in the dark ages of my occasionally misspent youth, when the legal drinking age in my home state of New York was 18 and minimum wage was less than a buck an hour, 30 cents would buy you a nice highball. Really.

"Highball." Then a common term for a simple mixed cocktail, now a quaint, anachronistic word. The highball of choice for my untrained young palate was rye and ginger. Four ounces of ginger ale and a shot of whatever rye the bartender poured into it. I wasn't into labels in those days. Even for the ginger ale.

But that was in the long ago. Through the latter third of the twentieth century, rye rarely came to mind for the average drinker, displaced by a sharp consumer detour toward—*the horror!*—vodka.

Rye wound up far down the list of brown spirits, peering up longingly at the lofty perches occupied by a river of bourbons, a sea of Scotches, a tsunami of blends.

But that didn't deter all rye distillers. After all, vodka wasn't always wildly popular. Bourbon had its down periods. So, as the twenty-first century dawned, the forgotten whiskey began signaling a rebound.

Such star bourbon makers as Jim Beam, Wild Turkey, Old Overholt, and Van Winkle began pushing their ryes. Old Potrero, lesser known but a must-have with rye aficionados, put several styles on the shelf, and Michter's, which has a whole range of ryes, made a huge comeback. Rittenhouse Rye was launched by the Continental Distilling Co. of Philadelphia after the repeal of Prohibition. Later, it was bought by Heaven Hill Distilleries, the nation's largest independent family-owned spirits producer and the second largest holder of aging American whiskey in the world. Kirstin Jackson, brand manager for Rittenhouse Rye Whiskey, didn't mind crowing a bit after Rittenhouse Bottled-In-Bond Rye Whisky took the title of "North American Whiskey of the Year" at the 2006 San Francisco World Spirits Competition.

"Historically, rye whiskey has been the ultimate expression of classic American whiskey style, and we at Heaven Hill Distilleries were one of only three remaining producers to keep the style alive during the lean years when rye was overshadowed by bourbon and Scotch and Irish whiskies," she said.

In the Present

It is difficult to find what one can confidently refer to as a "watershed year" in modern times when it comes to the expansion of the world of whiskey. Legislation, marketing and distribution practices, and economic cycles, of course, have all had their effects, but finding that one "Aha!" moment in so global a topic is a fool's errand.

That does not mean, however, that we cannot point to various events in the first decade of the twenty-first century that show the hold that brown spirits have on so much of the world's population, from academics to distillers to consumers. New products, new facilities, new research findings, and new directions abound.

In 2003, Wales got its first legal distillery when the new Penderyn facility began producing a single malt. The privately owned distillery, which operates in the Brecon Beacons National Park, thus revived a Welsh industry that had provided experienced whisky makers who, along with the Scots-Irish, were among the founding fathers of the American bourbon industry. In Penderyn, the American link lives on. Its whisky is first aged in used bourbon casks shipped from the United States before being finished in Wales in rare, used Madeira barrels.

In 2006, an obscure magazine called *Photonics Spectra*, published in Pittsfield, Massachusetts, in the heart of the Berkshire Mountains, reported that scientists at the University of Tennessee in Knoxville and at the U.S. Department of Agriculture Forest Service's Southern Research Station in Pineville, Louisiana, were busy "analyzing wood charcoal using mid-infrared spectroscopy. With the chemical information they gather, they hope to apply near-IR spectroscopy and other techniques for online process monitoring in the spirits industry."

Or, in plain English, which mercifully emerged several paragraphs later: "The manufacture of Tennessee whiskey is distinguished by the use of the Lincoln County Process, a days-long mellowing step in which the newly distilled spirit is filtered through a 10-foot-thick layer of charcoal made from sugar maple. Infrared spectroscopy offers distillers a means of verifying that the charcoal they produce for the process is of the proper species of maple. . . . Given the importance of tradition in the branding of spirits and the anecdotal evidence that suggests that the quality of Tennessee whiskey depends on the species of maple used to make the charcoal, there is a strong incentive for distillers to confirm that sugar maple is the source material,

explained Nicole Labbé, an assistant professor at the university's Tennessee Forest Products Center."

Also in 2006, the United Kingdom completed the circle of having at least one distillery in each of its component countries when England's first and only registered whisky distilling company, the English Whiskey Company at St. George's Distillery in Norfolk, was founded. It joined Wales' lone distillery—the aforementioned Penderyn—Northern Ireland's Bushmills, and the hundred-plus distilleries in Scotland as the United Kingdom lineup.

That same year, while most Scotch distilleries continued to work on ways to smooth out the peaty aromas and tastes of the popular whisky to broaden its market appeal, virtually no one was trying to make it have more kick. No one except the Bruichladdich Distillery on the Isle of Islay, off Scotland's west coast. It revived a centuries-old recipe for a 184 proof whisky—which means an astounding 92 percent alcohol.

Why?, you may ask. Me, too.

Bruichladdich Managing Director Mark Reynier was very straightforward about that: "We are only doing this because we have this ancient recipe and because we can. Our team can only get involved in the fun of recreating truly historic malts because we are independent—and we can."

The run began the week of February 27—at 11:30 in the morning, to be precise—and only twelve barrels of the quadruple-distilled single malt were produced, with master distiller Jim McEwan doing the honors.

Martin Martin, a seventeenth century travel writer of some renown, mentioned this particular whisky in his book, *The Western Islands of Scotland*.

" . . . The first taste affects all the members of the body: two spoonfuls of this last liquor is a sufficient dose; and if any man should exceed this, it would presently stop his breath, and endanger his life."

McEwan, a distiller of four decades' experience, said, "The whisky first ran at 92 percent, which will make an average of 90 percent. It is very similar to the whisky tasted by Martin all those years ago. It's very floral, but most importantly it most certainly takes your breath away!"

Bruichladdich (pronounced *brook-laddie*, Gaelic for a "raised beach") was built in 1881 by William Harvey and his brothers. It was closed in 1994 by its then-owner, Jim Beam Brands. It was purchased in 2000 by Mark Reynier, a wine merchant who headed a group of investors, and, after a spruce-up of the original Victorian equipment, it resumed distilling on May 29, 2001.

Then in 2007, places not known for producing whiskies got into the act. In France, the Distillerie Bertrand in the Alsatian village of Uberach was launched to make both single malts and blends. The micro-distillery boom took hold in America as craft facilities began popping up like toadstools after a spring rain, in New York, Alaska, Wyoming, and Virginia, to name just a few states. The

" "The whisky first ran at 92 percent, which will make an average of 90 percent. It is very similar to the whisky tasted by Martin all those years ago. It's very floral, but most importantly it most certainly takes your breath away!" "

BRUICHLADDICH
MCM
LXX
VII
'77/32

PROGRESSIVE
HEBRIDEAN
DISTILLERS

32 AGED YEARS
RARE 1977
ISLAY SINGLE MALT
SCOTCH WHISKY

700 ml
47.4 % Alc./Vol.

Murree Brewing Company of Pakistan, the only malt whisky distillery in the Muslim world, launched a 21-year-old single malt Scotch whisky. The catch is, Murree's product lines, which already included 8- and 12-year-old single malts, cannot legally be exported. And, by law, only members of Pakistan's tiny non-Muslim minority can obtain a permit to buy liquor for home consumption.

Of course, that doesn't prevent a black market trade in whiskies, especially from the Rawalpindi-based Murree firm whose chief executive, M.P. Bhandara, told the Associated Press, "Very few distilleries anywhere in the world, even the high-end ones in Scotland, produce 21-year-old malts." The Murree Brewery was established in 1861 to provide beer for occupying British troops, thus the "brewing" in the name. While it continues to brew beer, it has been making Scotch-style whisky since the early 1960s.

In 2008, a Scottish investors group thought so highly of the potential for profit in the industry that it announced the Glenglassaugh Distillery would be resuming production after a hiatus of twenty-two years. You may not think you've ever had any of its high-end Scotch whisky, but if you ever tried Cutty Sark, Famous Grouse, or Laing's made in 1986 or before, then you have. Glenglassaugh sold its product to those widely known companies for use in their blends. The distillery, built in 1875, is located in the village of Portsoy on the Moray coast of Scotland.

At about the same time, Chivas Brothers, the Scotch whisky and premium gin wing of Pernod Ricard, announced plans to expand its Glenlivet facility as well as re-open its Braeval Distillery that had been closed for six years. It was to be used to supply spirit for Chivas' blended whiskies.

In 2009, a spate of unusual whiskies hit the global market. One example was Octomore, another expression from those aforementioned iconoclastic Bruichladdich distillers. This one they claimed was the world's peatiest whisky; distilled from barley peated to 131 parts per million, which makes it three times peatier than any other whisky ever produced. They called it "an iron fist in a velvet glove."

Another example was Glengoyne Distillery's 40-year-old Highland Single Malt—just 250 crystal decanters, sold at US$4,552 each. Yet another was from William Grant & Sons Distillers Ltd., which released a half-century-old whisky it was selling for US$16,000 a bottle. The Glenfiddich 50 Year Old was limited to just five hundred numbered, hand-blown glass bottles decorated with Scottish silver and packaged in leather-bound cases. William Grant had aged only two casks of this particular single malt since the 1950s at its Dufftown, Scotland, facility. It became, by most reputable accounts, the second most expensive whisky ever. A 60-year-old Macallan sold for a little over US$10,000 in 1991 but today is valued at about US$40,000.

In 2010, Jim Murray's *Whisky Bible*, the UK top-selling such guide, shocked many people inside and outside the industry by naming 18-year-old Sazerac Rye from Kentucky the world's best whisky/ whiskey, elevating it beyond even the UK's beloved Scotches. It topped 3,850 other whiskies that were considered, with Ardbeg Supernova from the Hebridean island of Islay as No. 2 after dominating the awards for the three prior years. Interestingly, an Indian whisky, Amrut Fusin from Bangalore, was No. 3.

So, Off We Go

That, in a rather oversized nutshell, is the history of whiskey, writ broadly, touching some highlights and some lowlights, probably raising as many questions as it answers.

However, it provides a framework for what follows. For further illumination, the rest of this anthology contains essays from writers of various types who have delved into the people and products that have helped advance the cause of brown spirits around the globe through the centuries.

I recommend you sink into a comfortable armchair with a splash of your favorite whiskey close at hand and enjoy this trip through a world of dreamers and drams.

A BRIEF HISTORY *of* DISTILLING

BILL OWENS

To get a handle on why there are so many variations in whiskies yet so comparatively few ways to make them, it is helpful to understand the basic process everyone must use. And to boil that down to comprehensible verbiage, you need someone steeped in the art. Bill Owens has plenty of credentials. He was the founder of the American Distilling Institute in 2003, publisher of the magazines American Brewer *and* BEER: The Magazine, *founder of what is purported to be America's first brewpub (in Hayward, California, in 1982), and a mover and shaker in the current craft distilling movement. This explanation is contained in* The Art of Distilling Whiskey and Other Sports, *which he wrote and edited with Alan Dikty (Quarry Books, Beverly, Mass., 2009).*

Since the earliest known use of distillation about 5,000 years ago, practice of the art has grown and spread around the world in several waves, the speed and extent of each being dictated by geography, trade routes, and cultural and religious influences. Each successive wave gave rise to significant technical advances in distillation, making it less expensive, more efficient, and more controllable.

Possibly the first written record of distillation is in the "Epic of Gilgamesh," which describes a form of essential oil distillation practiced in Babylon as far back as 3000 B.C.E. Herbs were placed in a large heated cauldron of boiling water, and the cauldron's opening was covered with a sheepskin, fleece side down. Periodically the sheepskin was changed, and the condensate soaking the fleece was wrung out into a small jar. Essential oils floated to the surface of the water collected in the jar and were skimmed off. Medieval texts and woodcuts show the same principle being used to concentrate alcoholic vapors from boiling wine. Incidentally, this is similar in principle to a method the Phoenicians used for consuming cannabis.

"…alcohol distillation was an established industry in the ancient Indian area known as Taxila, in modern northwest Pakistan…"

By 500 B.C.E., alcohol distillation was an established industry in the ancient Indian area known as Taxila, in modern northwest Pakistan, where archaeologists discovered a perfectly preserved terra-cotta distillation system. In this process, steam rising from a pot of boiling water passed through a bed of fermented grains, picking up alcohol and flavors from the grains. The vapors then struck the bottom of a second pot, filled with cold water, where they condensed and dripped into a collection tube.

From Taxila, knowledge spread to the East and the West, and by 350 B.C.E., knowledge of the distilling process appeared in the writing of Aristotle in Greece and Sinedrius in Libya. The first arrival of distillation technology in China is misty, but by 25 C.E., bronze stills of similar design were being produced and used there.

By the end of the first millennium C.E., the practice of distillation had spread throughout northern Africa and the Middle East. The process had advanced significantly over this thousand-year period, and the material being distilled was now boiled directly in a large sealed pot, which had a long tube leading from its apex to a small collection jar. When the Moors invaded Spain, they brought this technology with them, and soon the genie (or spirit) was out of the bottle. The technology spread from Spain to Italy in 1100 C.E. and was recorded in Ireland by 1200, Germany by 1250, and France by 1300. England, Scotland, Poland, Russia and Sweden joined the club by 1400.

"European exploration and conquest spread rapidly around the world, carrying the technology of distillation with it."

European exploration and conquest spread rapidly around the world, carrying the technology of distillation with it. The first stills in the Americas appeared not long after the conquistadores, and the Portuguese brought the technology to Japan by 1500.

This technology was largely controlled by alchemists and monasteries, who continuously experimented and improved on the equipment. By the mid-1600s, several texts had been published on the subject of distillation, including "The Art of Distillation" by Jonathan French (1651). As this information spread beyond clerical and scientific circles, wealthy individuals began to establish still houses on their estates.

As knowledge blossomed through the Renaissance, distillation continued to develop rapidly. Distillation was removed from the exclusive province of scientists, monks and professionals and became a common household art. Recipe books abounded.

By the 1700s, the complexity and sophistication of commercial-scale distilling equipment advanced rapidly. Advances in the understanding of how distillation actually worked led to new still designs that could make better quality spirits more easily and faster than in the past. Distilling became more accessible to the masses, and the monopoly held by the church and the elite classes was threatened. These centers of power soon enacted restrictions, at first to protect that monopoly, and later purely for revenue.

Just as the appearance of microbreweries followed the renaissance of home brewing, increasing the choices and level of quality for all beer drinkers, microdistilleries are starting to thrive around the world, some using traditional equipment, but many using new equipment, methods and techniques developed by the newly liberated home distillers. Many of these modern small distilleries are experimenting with new types and categories of spirits, creating novel and sometimes uniquely local spirits.

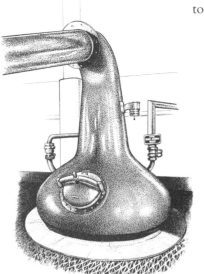

A modern industrial still

FROM SINGLE MALTS
— *to* —
FINE MARRIAGES

JAMES RODEWALD

Virtually all of the writers in the book admit that no one truly knows where the story of whiskey began; that's one of the unifying aspects of creating any history of whiskey. However, each has his favorites among the legends and the lore. Here, James Rodewald, former drinks editor of **Gourmet** *magazine and, as he puts it, a lover of whiskies sweet, smoky, and everywhere in between, offers his take on the history of the spirit.*

There are nearly as many legends about the origins of distillation as there are primitive cultures. The most common claim is that the Babylonians of Mesopotamia discovered the process some 2,000 years before the birth of Christ. China also has been credited with the invention, during the Eastern Han period (C.E. 25–220), as has India around 150 B.C.E. There are those who speculate that ancient Egyptians and Assyrians practiced the art. Intriguingly, recent scholarship points to the possibility of pre-Hispanic distillation (of mescal) in the Valley of Colima, Mexico, as early as 1500–1000 B.C.E. But all these claims are, frankly, pretty dubious.

Some of the confusion is probably linguistic. For example, *distillare* is used by several classical authors, but always to mean "to drop" or "to drip" (as in snow, or the nose of a cold sufferer), and some overzealous historians may have let their lust for liquor overwhelm the facts. Another natural mistake is to assume that when an explorer comes upon a new beverage and pronounces it "strong" that means it's been distilled. More likely he wants his dainty royal sponsor to believe he has never before indulged in such heavy-duty intoxicants. But if, for example, you've only tasted Budweiser, your first sip of a Belgian ale will certainly rattle your skull. Yet both are beers; neither is distilled.

Leaving aside the sexy speculation for a moment, what evidence there is points to Alexandria in the first century C.E. as being the birthplace of what we think of as distillation. That said, the chemists of that time were much more interested in precious metals than they were in potent potables. In fact, it's extremely unlikely that alcoholic beverages were distilled before the eleventh century. There is no question that the principles of distillation were known long before then, but antiquarian happy hour options were likely limited to relatively low alcohol beverages like mead, wine, beer, *pulque* and other regional specialties. And that was probably fine and dandy at the time. It also was, it must be said, quite an achievement. Like the first person to eat an oyster, you've got to admire the character of someone willing to drink what is, after all, essentially the result of controlled spoilage.

The earliest tipplers were probably Sumerians. They are believed to be the first humans to trade a nomadic lifestyle for agriculture, and their primary crop was barley. Based on archeological evidence, one of the many things they made with the grain was a fermented beverage. Making beer requires that the grain be "malted," which is to say sprouted and its germination cut short by drying, to convert some of the starch into a fermentable sugar. How the Sumerians accomplished that isn't known for sure, but they lived in a flood plain between the lower Tigris and Euphrates rivers and it's certainly possible that an accident of nature caused their barley to sprout and, not wanting to lose their harvest, they did what they could to dry it out, thus arresting its growth. Perhaps the malted barley then fermented naturally. Here again there are any number of speculative scenarios, but the most important thing for our purposes, as the late, great whisky writer Michael Jackson wrote in his *Complete Guide to Single Malt Scotch*, "To grow barley, transform it into malt and then into beer, is halfway towards the making of whisky."

Halfway, but still a long way. The first written reference to distillation of malted barley occurs in 1494, when the Scottish Exchequer records duty paid on "eight bolls of malt" to make *aqua vitae* for King James IV. That would have been enough grain to make somewhere in the range of 1,000 liters of distillate, a considerable quantity, but still probably not whisky as we think of it. The most likely use for this "water of life" was alchemy. James, in addition to possessing great surgical skills and medical knowledge, was an ardent supporter of the alchemical arts. His treasurer recorded many expenditures for "*aqua vitae* to the *quinta essencia*," the latter being the alchemist's Holy Grail. John Small, writing in *Sketches of Early Scottish Alchemists* in 1875, says *quinta essencia* "should convert other metals into pure gold, heal all diseases, and prolong human life far beyond its ordinary bounds." After James's death, in 1513, references to such *aqua vitae* purchases cease. The inevitable conclusion is that those famous bolls of malt were not destined to warm the cockles of ordinary Scotsmen.

As compelling as that first piece of documentation has been to chroniclers of Scotch whisky history, a much more important event occurred forty years later, when King Henry VIII began the systematic suppression of the English monasteries. Monks had been growing crops, brewing beer from their grain, making wine from their grapes and mead from their honey, and distilling various fruits, berries, and grains for medicinal and alchemical purposes to great effect within the cloister. Cast out into secular society, they naturally turned to the skills they had acquired earlier.

Fernand Braudel, one of the twentieth century's most important historians, wrote that "the great innovation, the revolution in Europe, was the appearance of brandy and spirits made from grain—in a word: alcohol. The sixteenth century created it; the seventeenth consolidated it; the eighteenth popularized it."

For farmers, the ability to convert the fruits of their labor into something that wouldn't spoil, was always in demand, and could be transported more easily than the raw material was a godsend. These farmers would sell their unaged spirit to passersby, or perhaps sell barrels of it to local hotels or to wine and spirits merchants. Early Scotch whisky would've been pretty rough stuff—aging in wood casks didn't begin until the early nineteenth century—and it was often flavored with fruit, herbs or spices and often used as the base of a toddy. But it was still popular enough to catch the attention of the Scottish Parliament, which imposed duties on both malt and the spirit made from it in the middle of the seventeenth century. When Scotland signed the Act of Union, in 1707, with England, its parliament was dissolved and taxes and enforcement were imposed and executed by England. Needless to

A distillery in Scotland

say, the Kingdom of Great Britain asked for larger and larger slices of the whisky pie, leading to a series of uprisings in Scotland and pushing its distillers underground—and practically underwater. Sea caves were popular spots for illegal stills.

The onerous taxes and absurd, ever-changing restrictions placed on legal distilleries made it impossible for them to create a product that could compete with the outlaw product on price or quality. The whisky coming out of the small, illicit stills was far superior to most of the sanctioned product. As Gavin D. Smith writes in *The Secret Still: Scotland's Clandestine Whisky Makers*, "As duty levels on legal distillation were raised, the illicit trade became even more attractive as an occupation. Legal distilleries such as Ardbeg on Islay [the most southerly island of the inner Hebrides] went bankrupt because of the increases in duty coupled with illegal activity nearby."

Finally, acting on the recommendations of a committee formed to study the state of its spirits industry, Britain instituted the Excise Act of 1823. The Act greatly increased fines for illegal distilling, but it also cut duties and allowed for smaller batch sizes (to improve quality). Quality improved, and the seeds of a sustainable industry were sown.

The invention in the mid-1800s of a still that could operate continuously without having to be cleaned between batches made industrial-scale production of grain whisky possible; the older pot still had to be emptied and cleaned after each use. This soon gave rise to an entirely new business: blending.

Combining the more flavorful single malts with lighter and less expensive grain whisky may have started as a way to stretch the more expensive ingredient, but the lighter, more quaffable result found an enthusiastic audience. Before they began blending and selling whisky, the Chivas Brothers, George Ballantine and John Walker all were grocers; John Dewar and Arthur Bell were wine and spirits merchants. Remarkably, all the brands that bear their names still are going strong. In fact, blends today soak up roughly 90 percent of malt whisky production, and those blends made up nearly 93 percent of the whisky market in 2009. Despite the category's déclassé image, blends can be every bit as complex and delicious as single malts. John Glaser, a Minnesotan, left his marketing director job at Johnnie Walker to start a company dedicated to blending malts, grains, and malts with grains. He established Compass Box in 2000, and his influence on the industry has been disproportionate to the small number of bottles he produces.

While single malts represent a fraction of total sales, and despite the continuing consolidation of the Scotch whisky industry (in 2009, four multinational companies owned 62 percent of the distillation capacity for malt whisky and 85 percent of the distillation capacity for grain whisky), malt maniacs can rejoice in the knowledge that the trend toward "premiumization" continues. While there have been plenty of marketing-driven bottlings that told a nice story but failed to deliver in the glass, there have been far more fascinating and worthwhile releases in recent years. Glenmorangie Finealta, for example, is a re-creation of a 1903 recipe in which the malted barley was dried over peat fires, a practice that the distillery does not employ in its regular bottlings. And this from a distillery owned by the French luxury giant Louis Vuitton-Moët Hennessy. At the opposite extreme is Kilchoman, the first farm distillery to be built on Islay in more than 120 years and one of the smallest distilleries in the country. A sample of its unaged spirit, tasted just days off the still in 2006, was incredibly impressive: complex, rich and deliciously smoky. Recent aged releases have attracted the attention of whisky lovers, and its summer 2010 release was named Artisan Whisky of the Year by *Malt Advocate* magazine.

The two companies have little in common, other than that they're making delicious single malts. And that is, after all, what matters most.

The GIANTS of THEIR TIMES

no. 2

In any field of human endeavor, there are the giants, the pioneers on whose shoulders stand those who come after them.

In the world of whiskey, there arguably are no greater names than George Smith, Jack Daniel, the Irish titans, the sprawling Beam clan, and many others.

These are their stories, told by experts in the field.

GEORGE SMITH

GEORGE SMITH
— and —
THE GLENLIVET

F. PAUL PACULT

While most parts of the world enthusiastically support their local distilled spirits, Scotland arguably is the most storied, most imitated, and most written-about of all whisky regions. In reality, whisky making in its mist-shrouded Highlands, Speyside, and islands didn't really come into its own as an export until the nineteenth century. That, writes the prolific author F. Paul Pacult—a member of the Bourbon Hall of Fame and the Keepers of the Quaich (also known as the Scotch Malt Whisky Society)—in his book A Double Scotch: How Chivas Regal and The Glenlivet Became Global Icons *(John Wiley & Sons Inc., 2005), stems largely from the talent and efforts of one George Smith, born in the Glenlivet area of Scotland in 1792.*

Recognized as one of highland Scotland's most dazzling and bucolic river valleys, Glenlivet was a famous location long before The Glenlivet whisky was invented and became an enduring symbol of its place of origin. Glenlivet, or *Gleann-liobh-aite* in Gaelic, means "valley of the smooth flowing one."

In the late winter of 1792 what Andrew Smith's infant son George could not have known was that he was born in the epicenter of a monumental social earthquake. At its core, this deep-rooted upheaval concerned what the average Scotsman perceived to be his right to distill whisky unfettered by governmental interference, regulation or taxation. Secluded, remote Glenlivet felt the seismic shudder more than most other places. What took place in Glenlivet over George Smith's lifetime sent political tremors across the whole of Britain, including deep within the walls of Parliament.

"... George Smith would initiate his own personal earthquake within Scotland's whisky trade."

Moreover, 32 years after his birth, George Smith would initiate his own personal earthquake within Scotland's whisky trade. Andrew Smith could never have guessed that his fourth son would end up being instrumental in totally altering the landscape of whisky making in Scotland, changing it to the extent that even George's neighbors in the glen would turn into mortal enemies. Andrew Smith would die before his son became the most famous whisky distiller in all of Scotland.

A turbulent era of whisky smuggling and illicit distilling in Scotland began roughly 150 years before George Smith's birth at Upper Drumin and lasted nearly two centuries. The period from 1760 to 1849, in particular, proved to be the apex of illegal distilling activity. The seed of the problem was planted in the mid-17th Century when the Scottish Parliament passed the Internal Act of Excyse on January 31, 1644. That legislation put Scotland's farmer-distillers on official notice that the distilling of whisky was no longer a free, uncontrolled exercise. The Act of Excyse "... imposed a duty of 2s. 8d. on 'everie pynt of aquavytie or strong watteris sold within the countrye'," according to whisky author

Gavin D. Smith in his book "The Scottish Smuggler" (2003). The "2s. 8d." meant a duty of two shillings and eight pence to be paid on each pint of *uisge beatha*. In the 1600s, a "pynt" equaled roughly one-third of a gallon.

The overwhelming majority of 17th Century whisky distillers were ordinary farmers and subtenants who led hand-to-mouth existences within the trap of an archaic, yet effective, feudal system. For the most part, the farmer-distillers were simply dealing with excess volumes of bere, Scotland's ubiquitous and vigorous four-row barley. Not only did distillation wisely utilize harvest surpluses of barley, it afforded the farmer-distillers a useful mode of currency or trade as well as a salable product that was growing in popularity. The imposition of a governmentally generated duty, then, came as a serious blow to their otherwise sturdy sensibilities. The Act of Excyse was an insult.

But as history would depict, the Act of Excyse was just the launch, the initial volley, one might say, of what was destined to become a long, bitterly contested tradition of continual governmental meddling with whisky distillation. Over succeeding centuries, Scotch whisky would become the favorite duty target, a taxable pawn and cash cow of both the Scottish and English Parliaments to help finance potential wars, to pay the debts incurred by past conflicts on foreign soils or to bail out Parliament when monies were mismanaged.

Meanwhile, whisky's popularity all across Scotland hurtled forward. This dramatic growth in consumption happened, in one part, because so much whisky was then being distilled in both cities and the countryside and, in another part, by the natural allure of whisky's mysterious nature. The native strong ale fermented from barley was turbid in appearance and spotty in quality. Its appeal to the masses was waning by the close of the 17th Century. Scots, in general, were ready to glom onto a new potable.

Scotland's first large distillery, Ferintosh, founded in the 1660s and owned by Duncan Forbes of Culodden, produced the nation's first brand of whisky of the same name. Though the distillery, located in Ross-shire, was burned to the ground in the Jacobite insurrection of 1689, Forbes, who was fiercely anti-Jacobite, rebuilt Ferintosh, which was one of Scotland's first industrial complexes and proved to be a forerunner of modern whiskies.

[In the early 1800s] though the tide was starting to turn against smuggling, illicit whisky received an unexpected and unintentional boost from none other than George IV, King of Great Britain. During a much-ballyhooed royal visit to Scotland in August 1822, word got out that the King had become smitten with whisky, in particular the highly respected illicit variety produced in or around Glenlivet.

Wrote Elizabeth Grant in "Memoirs of a Highland Lady 1797–1830," her period tome, "The whole country went mad. Everybody strained every point to get to Edinburgh to receive him. Sir Walter Scott and the Town Council were overwhelming themselves with the preparation. . . . Lord Conyngham, the Chamberlain, was looking everywhere for pure Glenlivet whisky; the King drank nothing else. It was not to be had out of the Highlands. My father sent word to me—I was the cellarer—to empty my pet bin, where was whisky long in wood, long in uncorked bottles, mild as milk. . . . Much as I grudged this treasure it made our fortunes afterwards, showing on what trifles great events depend."

The King's supposed appreciation of smuggler's whisky instigated a national awareness of the superior quality of whisky from Glenlivet, which became something of a brand name for better smugglers' whisky. This wide recognition catapulted forward the mystique of Scotland's most famous glen, even though doubtless much of the illicit whisky touted as "Glenlivet" was produced in other areas of the Highlands. His admiration of Glenlivet also led him to instruct his Home Secretary, Robert Peel, to request the Board of Excise that they exercise clemency to smugglers. George IV clearly didn't want his whisky supply to be cut off.

The Upper Drumin lease was set to expire in 1823. To complicate matters for George Smith, his landlord, the Duke of Gordon, was experiencing serious financial difficulties due in part to the dishonesty of his factor, or estate foreman, William Mitchell [who embezzled] £3,200 from the Duke, a staggering sum for the day. James Skinner, a sound and reputable young man with superb management skills, replaced Mitchell in 1823. Making his case to retain at least part of Upper Drumin under the new management, George proposed that he and a friend, Peter Fraser, share the task. George's primary, if visionary, line of reasoning was that the Upper Drumin property could support a proper, licensed malt whisky distillery—a legal distillery that could produce larger volumes of superior whisky than the small bothies that dotted Glenlivet's countryside. The production of legal whisky would favorably affect the glen's barley farmers, George reasoned. Perhaps the opening of one legal distillery would even stimulate further interest within the Glenlivet community to swap smuggling for lawful distilling.

Since George was of sound character as well as industrious and smart, Skinner quickly consented. George agreed to pay the Duke the annual sum of £9, while Peter Fraser agreed to pay £18. Green, hilly Upper Drumin was secured for the next two decades.

George began producing fresh spirit sometime in the winter of 1825. Highland whisky in 1825 was sold unaged and raw, frequently in 10-gallon casks referred to as "ankers." George's two pot stills were at least large enough to meet the legal minimum of 40 gallons as specified by the Excyse Act. Smugglers' pot stills, smaller and cruder, were no match in terms of volume for a pair of full-time pot stills. As George's fame grew, the ire of the smugglers against him escalated. An atmosphere of retribution hung over the glen like laden springtime clouds.

When rumors circulated that some other reformed Glenlivet smugglers . . . were pondering going legitimate, blatant threats were made to their faces. Suspicious fires destroyed several upstart legal distilleries throughout the Highlands. Years later in a newspaper interview, George Smith described the hazardous years of 1824, 1825 and 1826 in Glenlivet: "When the new Act was heard of in Glenlivet and in the Highlands of Aberdeenshire, they [the smugglers] ridiculed the idea that anyone should be found daring enough to start distilling in their midst. . . . The desperate character of the smugglers and the violence of their threats deterred anyone for some time. At length in 1824, I, George Smith, who was then a robust young fellow, and not given to be easily 'fleggit,' determined to chance it. I was already a tenant of the Duke and received every encouragement from his grace and his factor Mister Skinner. The outlook was an ugly one, though. I was warned by my civil neighbors that they [smugglers] meant to burn the new distillery to the ground and me in the heart of it."

An unexpected whisky glut in late 1826 and 1827 undercut the meager gains made by George in his first full year of operation. George's financial situation had become so dire by March 1827 that he was forced to turn down a barley delivery that was already paid for. The alarmed Skinner, a fervent advocate of both legal distilling and of George's distillery at Upper Drumin, revealed in [a] March 8 letter to Reverend John Anderson [the Duke of Gordon's commissioner for financial and legal matters], "George commenced the Business the First in the Country under every disadvantage. He was not the master of his business, legal distillation requiring much greater care than the System of Smuggling to extract the quantity of Spirits required by Law from the grain. He commenced, as he now admits, when he was upwards of £100 behind and had about £300 to lay out in utensils and houses upon credit. And from want of money to go to Market for his grain was obliged to buy at Disadvantage. . . . I am sorry to mention that [Smith] has become so embarrassed in his circumstances that he has intimated to me he will be unable to go on."

"George's financial situation had become so dire by March 1827 that he was forced to turn down a barley delivery that was already paid for."

In actions that depict the seriousness of the situation, Anderson responded to Skinner via letter on March 9. After discussing not only George's predicament but likewise the welfare of local barley farmers and greater Glenlivet in general, Anderson and the Duke decided to financially bail out George. Without the intervention, aid and encouragement of James Skinner, the Reverend John Anderson and the 4th Duke of Gordon in the spring of 1827, George would have been left no choice but to close Drumin Glenlivet. If that had happened whisky drinkers in later decades would never have known the seductive whisky made by the greatest of all the Speyside distillers.

Smuggling in the Scottish Lowlands had been virtually stamped out by 1827, but in the Highlands it continued. In 1868, George Smith, in an interview in the *London Scotsman*, recalled: "The Laird of Aberlour [fellow legitimate distiller James Gordon] had presented me with a pair of hair-trigger pistols for ten guineas, and they were never out of my belt for years. I got together two or three stout fellows for servants, armed them with pistols, and let it be known everywhere that I would fight for my place to the last shot. I had a good character as a man of my word and, through watching by turns every night for years, we contrived to save the distillery from the fate so freely predicted for it. But I often, both at kirk [church] and market had rough times of it among the glen people; and if it had not been for the Laird of Aberlour's pistols, I don't think I should be telling you this story now. . . . The country was in a desperately lawless state at this time."

> *"'I got together two or three stout fellows for servants, armed them with pistols, and let it be known everywhere that I would fight for my place to the last shot.'"*

By 1867, when George Smith turned 75, The Glenlivet malt whisky had become so closely identified with its creator that mentioning one almost automatically meant inclusion of the other. In outlandishly brazen attempts to hitch their whisky wagons to that of the most famous distillery in the Highlands, other distillers started to identify their whisky in part as "Glenlivet" by tacking on the place name to their own proprietary distillery name. Concerned about the rash of shameless mimics, the Smiths [George and his son John Gordon] began to voice concern about the growing confusion in the marketplace about what was and what wasn't the "real Glenlivet." The random and, in their eyes, fraudulent use of the word "Glenlivet" by malt whisky distillers who were not located in or even near Glenlivet was muddying the waters. The Smiths decided to make public their awareness of any Highland distillers who were misrepresenting their whiskies at the expense of The Glenlivet. [They] paid for the following advertisement that appeared in the liquor trade publication *Wine Trade Review* in 1868:

"Glenlivet Whisky. Messers. George & John Gordon Smith of The Glenlivet Distillery beg to intimate that Glenlivet is a district which belongs exclusively to his Grace the Duke of Richmond, and their Distillery was the First, and is *now* the Only Licensed Distillery in Glenlivet; and they respectfully caution the Trade and the public against other manufacturers of spirits offering the productions of their distilleries under the name of 'Glenlivet Whisky.' Finely matured and new whisky in casks any size; and by Messers. Andrew Usher & Co., West Nicholson Street, Edinburgh. Sole Agents South of the Tay [river]."

In the September 19, 1868, edition of the *London Scotsman,* an obviously enchanted reporter [with a relaxed spelling style] breathlessly observed, "There is hardly a public house in Scotland or England which does not announce for retail the 'finest Glenlivat whisky pure from the still.' . . . There is but one Allah, and Mahomet is his prophet. There is but one Glenlivet, and George Smith . . . is its distiller."

JACK DANIEL:
A Small Man Becomes a Giant

PETER KRASS

*Jack Daniel is one of the most ubiquitous names in the
whiskey business, as well as one of the most misunderstood.
The name often is referred to in the plural because the
company's label reads Jack Daniel's (a possessive, not a
plural). This Tennessee sipping whiskey is often confused with
bourbon, but it is not a bourbon because it is made using a
charcoal filtration process. Those things aside, the life and
legend of the man who spent his entire life in the environs
of tiny, rural Lynchburg, Tennessee, from 1849 to 1911 far
outstrips geography and time. In his biography* Blood &
Whiskey: The Life and Times of Jack Daniel *(John
Wiley & Sons, Inc., 2004), noted business biographer Peter
Krass overcomes the paucity of written records about and
correspondence to Jack Daniel to re-create a fascinating life. In
this excerpt, we meet Jack Daniel just after the Civil War, a
sixteen-year-old orphan taken in by Dan Call, a prosperous
local farmer and shopkeeper who operated a distillery with the
help of his former slave Uncle Nearis Green.*

For Lincoln County distillers like Dan Call and Uncle Nearis
Green, there was one absolutely crucial step before the
whiskey was poured into the wooden kegs: it was filtered
through pulverized charcoal made from the sugar maple tree. This

became known as the Lincoln County Process. Some distillers had been sweetening their whiskey with maple sugar, but at some point someone decided to experiment with sugar maple charcoal, both to filter out any impurities and to capture a hint of sweetness—just a hint, because the charcoal itself has no distinct flavor.

According to legend, it was the Lynchburg pioneer Alfred Eaton who invented the process in the 1820s. Others say this signature technique was handed down by slaves who distilled whiskey in the hills. The most important piece of lore, for big drinkers, is that this mellowing process magically takes the hog tracks—the hangover—out of the whiskey.

As the whiskey trickled through the charcoal, Uncle Nearis and Jack poured some into charred barrels for aging and some into jugs for immediate consumption. A portion of the spent stillage was saved for the next batch, while the remainder went to the pigs and the cattle. This beer served as excellent stock feed. Old geezers hanging around the still houses always got a hoot out of watching the pigs stagger about and squeal after gluttonously inhaling the feed with a kick. And a kick was what Dan Call and Jack Daniel wanted to give their customers, too; their whiskey would become renowned for being a big bruiser, a whiskey in which delicious flavors of maple, malt, rye, and, of course, corn did battle.

Jack was in love. He was in love with Dan Call's still, a great companion to an orphaned young man. The taste of the burning maple on his tongue, the smoke filling his lungs and giving him substance, the sour mash tempering the sweetness, and even the sharp sting of the "white dog" all created an experience he immersed himself in.

Jack was embarking on a noble adventure, rooted in traditions handed down by his forefathers in Ireland and Scotland. Whiskey distilling was a symbol of their fight against oppressive governments—on both sides of the Atlantic. Whiskey distilling was a means for Jack,

who embodied that independent fighting spirit of his ancestors, to recapture the glorious past.

While Uncle Nearis remained in command of the still, the charismatic sixteen-year-old Jack became the quintessential salesman. In contrast to Dan, who had been content to sell the whiskey at his general store alone, his protégé was obsessively intent on expanding their market. Jack would load the jugs into a mule-drawn wagon and peddle their whiskey to stores and individuals in the surrounding villages of Lois, Lynchburg, Mulberry, and County Line, among others.

Although always quick to greet customers with a friendly wave and a joke, inside Jack was burning to break out of the backwoods. As he traveled around the county, he witnessed many who had prospered before the war now struggling in comparative poverty and mired in much bitterness and apathy, to which he didn't want to fall prey. He discovered that he wanted more for himself than what this rather modest market would yield. The boy distiller, as he'd soon be known due to his diminutive stature and youthful looks, set his sights on the

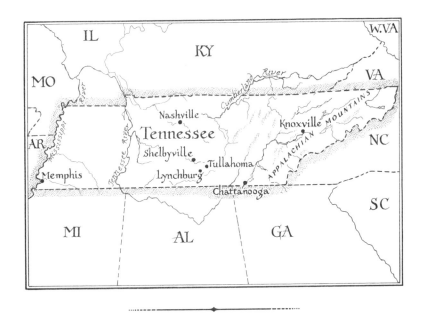

big city. If Jack could peddle enough whiskey, he could buy his own farm, build a superior distillery, and live the good life.

Some of the whiskey being sold was hardly whiskey. The liquor sold to the Indians was cut with whatever was handy—burnt sugar, oil, paint, Jamaican ginger, red pepper, and patent medicines—all for the effect of coloring, flavor, and profit.

Now, while Jack wasn't peddling Rotgut, Red Dynamite, Skull-bending Lightning, Coffin Varnish, or Kickapoo Jubilee Juice, among dozens of other variations on the name for "strong water," to Indians, untold dangers lurked where he intended to venture with his whiskey: Huntsville, Alabama. A good fifty-mile journey south, on the strategic Tennessee River, it was an expanding marketplace wallowing in sin—a city where man drank whiskey one-half of the time and fought the other half. When a Huntsville Baptist minister declared he would preach against liquor, a crowd attacked his church. That was 1848 and not much had changed by the latter 1860s. It was perfect.

The madcap Huntsville trips would become the stuff of family lore, which he prepared for with the slyness of a Rebel smuggler. Although Jack's pint size and baby face—he looked more like ten years old than he did sixteen—worked to his advantage in protecting him from a criminal element that was less likely to attack a boy, he was certainly exhibiting personal mettle, the kind of courage that was in his patriot grandfather's blood and in the Civil War veteran Dan Call's, because the dangers Jack faced were all too real. In addition to marauders and unscrupulous federal soldiers, there was the revenue man—or the *revenooer*, the derogatory name for government tax collectors—to contend with. Yes, Jack's diligent camouflaging of the whiskey strongly suggested that he was hiding it from not just landlocked pirates but also from the excise tax man, who had made an ignominious return. In 1862, the Lincoln administration had imposed an excise tax on a number of goods to pay for the war and created the office of the Commissioner of Internal Revenue to oversee collection efforts.

One of the great mysteries surrounding Jack Daniel is whether he, along with Dan, was indeed a moonshiner in the first years after the war. More specifically, when did Jack actually first register a distillery with the government, whether it was his own or one owned jointly with Dan? Was he first in line to register in 1866 when the federal tax revenue officers came calling, as legend has it? The answer is a resounding *no*; neither Jack nor Dan had a registered distillery in the years immediately following the war. The tradition of distilling—of moonshining—far outweighed any laws. And the most definitive piece of evidence: their names do not appear in the meticulously kept court records that noted legitimate business activity, including the local distillers.

Ultimately, the charismatic temperance leadership of the early 1880s did take its toll on Moore County distillers. Dan Call wasn't the only one to quit the business; by 1886, the number of registered distillers fell from twenty-three to fifteen. By the end of 1887, there would be only three fully operational Moore County whiskey manufacturers left standing: Tolley Brothers in Lynchburg, John Eaton County Line, and Jack Daniel.

As Jack watched the more timorous men shutter their distilleries, he realized that the downturn provided an opportunity for the bold. The time was ripe for expansion, and he was determined to fill the void by building a distillery that could compete with the like of Tolley & Eaton and the Robertson County boys. As for the location, he knew exactly where he wanted to be: in the heart of Lynchburg, both the center of the county's attention and strategically located to access distribution points in all four directions on the compass. The precise location: the hallowed Cave Spring, where the legendary Alfred Eaton had established the area's first distillery and allegedly discovered that leaching whiskey through charcoal mellowed and purified it of verdi gris and fusel oils. It was a magical place.

Just on the outskirts of Lynchburg proper, separated from the town square by a swath of trees, was a hollow with a rugged ravine running several hundred yards before abruptly meeting a limestone cliff. At the base was a cave, from which a cool draft of air blew and a stream of sparkling water bubbled forth like the mythic fountain of youth. With dense foliage veiling the cave's mouth, moss clinging to the rocks, and humidity hanging in the air, it was a Garden of Eden. It was a fairyland where the Scottish little people and Irish leprechauns played in the underbrush. The same mystical qualities that enshrouded what would become known as The Hollow, Jack wanted for his whiskey. He had to have it—only it belonged to the firm of Hiles & Berry, whose still on this property sat dormant.

The two partners were reluctant to part with the historic property, but they were moving along in years and were scaling back their activities. Finally, they decided to hold a trustees sale. On June 16, 1884, those interested in bidding on the 142-acre property gathered to survey The Hollow. After the preview, the bidding was opened. Not to be outbid or outclassed, Jack offered the winning figure of $2,180.40—a far more modest price than if the market had been booming. It would become a priceless piece of property.

Never one to twiddle his thumbs, Jack immediately erected a brick distillery and a one-room office building with a creaky front porch, which was easily mistaken for a shack. Fearful of compromising quality and of overextending himself in an uncertain market, he prudently kept his capacity at 150 gallons a day.

Shortly after he was operational, a reporter working for Goodspeed Brothers, a Nashville publishing house hell-bent on producing a monumental county-by-county history of Tennessee, toured Moore County. When the book was published in 1886, Jack was featured, with the writer noting that the Jack Daniel Distillery "has the capacity of fifty bushels per day and turns out some of the finest brands of 'Lincoln County' whiskey. Mr. Daniel is the owner of a large and productive farm, which he manages in connection with his distillery, and on which he raises large numbers of livestock." The surrounding land was "teeming with thousands of horses, mules, cattle, sheep and hogs," but Jack's prize livestock consisted of a herd of cattle—beneficiaries of the stillage—grazing in the undulating verdant pastures that graced each side of The Hollow.

One of the few Moore County men to receive a brief biographical sketch in the voluminous book, Jack had secured a preeminent status in a few short years.

JOHN JAMESON

JOHN POWER

The

IRISH WHISKEY TITANS

MALACHY MAGEE

*For a small country with only a small number of distilleries,
Ireland's spirit is known as widely as any other style.
Two of the legendary distillers whose names still adorn
their whiskies were John Jameson—who actually was from
Scotland—and John Power, both of whom receive prominent
inclusion in* Irish Whiskey: A 1000 Year Tradition,
*by Malachy Magee (Irish American Book Co., Dublin,
Reprinted 1998), for their work in building the foundation
of a lasting industry.*

The father figure of the Irish distilling trade is surely John Jameson. "Old John," as he came to be affectionately known, was a shrewd Scot who arrived in Dublin in the 1770s and subsequently founded one of the world's great whiskey houses.

The famous Bow Street distillery was already established in a small way when he bought himself a share of the business. By the year 1800 he had acquired full control and introduced his two sons to the business, John Jameson & Son Ltd.

John was well connected in the whiskey trade. His wife was a member of the Haig family, one of the oldest and most illustrious of the Scotch whisky houses, one of whose chairmen was Douglas Earl Haig, commander-in-chief of the British forces in France during World War I.

John's eldest son, also John, became owner of the Bow Street distillery, and the second son, William, ran the Marrowbone Lane distillery, previously owned by John Stein, a member of the well-known Scottish distilling family. Another Jameson brother was associated with a distillery near Enniscorthy, County Wexford, whose daughter married Giuseppe Marconi, and their son was the inventor of wireless telegraphy.

Old John was a stern and resolute man of high ideals. He impressed his employees that they would be well paid, with the best possible working conditions. In return for all these benefits their task would be to produce the finest whiskey in the world.

The Bow Street distillery grew in size and stature, eventually covering several acres of ground. John Jameson employed the highest skills in distillation, used the best equipment available and bought only the finest materials, paying the highest prices for the best Irish barley.

He invested immense capital in laying down great quantities of whiskey in sherry casks, to repose for many years in the dark vaults, so necessary in order to achieve that body and flavor which, John insisted, must excel all others.

The bonded warehouses of the Jameson distillery, long cloister-like avenues stacked with casks of aging whiskey, ran deep under the city of Dublin. At any given time more than two million gallons of whiskey were slowly maturing.

Production at the Bow Street distillery ceased in 1971 and was transferred to the John Power distillery at John's Lane pending the ultimate move to the new Midleton complex in County Cork. Members of the Jameson family have been associated with the company in an unbroken line for the past 200 years.

The last of the great whiskey houses to cease operations in Dublin was John Power & Son Ltd., in John's Lane, established in 1791. Although the renowned Power's Gold Label brand continues to be produced in Midleton in still greater quantities, and with all the meticulous care that has made it the top-selling whiskey in Ireland,

"John Jameson employed the highest skills in distillation, used the best equipment available and bought only the finest materials, paying the highest prices for the best Irish barley."

the dismantling in 1976 of the famous distillery regretfully signaled the end of a centuries-old Dublin tradition.

The distillery was set up by James Power, but it was his son and successor, John, a man of infinite energy and ability, who extended and eventually rebuilt the premises, covering over six acres, and incorporating the most up-to-date equipment. The workforce of nearly 300 enjoyed excellent conditions of employment.

"The company pioneered the use of miniature bottles—the famous 'Baby Power'—for which special government legislation had to be passed."

The site of the original distillery was occupied by a hostelry, owned by James Power, from which the mail coaches departed for the north and west of Ireland.

Sir John Power, as he became, initiated many developments in the industry. The company pioneered the use of miniature bottles—the famous "Baby Power"—for which special government legislation had to be passed. The distillery also was the first to bottle its own whiskey, the common practice then being to sell the produce in bulk to wholesalers and retailers. The first steam engine erected in Ireland was installed in the distillery, as also was the first dynamo to supply electric current in Dublin.

Sir John Power was made High Sheriff of Dublin, and on September 23, 1854, he laid the foundation stone for the magnificent O'Connell Monument in Dublin.

Alfred Barnard, to whose diligence we owe much of our

information about Irish distilleries of the past, was highly impressed with his visit to the John's Lane distillery, the spacious layout, the machinery and equipment and the general air of efficiency. He regarded it as "far superior to many I have seen throughout the United Kingdom, as complete a work as is possible to find anywhere."

The Still House held five large pot stills "all kept as bright and keen as burnished gold." There were 17 bonded warehouses within the complex, and the company had additional bonded stores in the basement of the then-new railway at Westland Row.

Barnard referred glowingly to the great engine rooms, the boiler house, the model stalls for the splendid shire horses, the harness room and the "horse hospital," or special sick boxes; the coach houses all were well-equipped and maintained with meticulous care; the handsome building fronting Thomas Street led into spacious public and private offices, dining rooms and visitors rooms.

At lunch in the distillery, Barnard sampled some special old Powers which, he said, was finer than anything he had ever tasted. "Perfect in flavour and as pronounced in the ancient aromas of Irish whiskey, so dear to the hearts of connoisseurs, as one could possibly desire."

JIM BEAM

The
UBIQUITOUS BEAMS

CHARLES K. COWDERY

There are many familiar names of long standing in the history of whiskey, but, the name Beam arguably overshadows all others in that world when it comes to family lineage, product quality, and global sales. Spirits chronicler Charles K. Cowdery, who created Made and Bottled in Kentucky, *the definitive public television documentary about the Bluegrass State's whiskey heritage, is thoroughly convinced of that. In his book* Bourbon, Straight: The Uncut and Unfiltered Story of American Whiskey *(published by Made and Bottled in Kentucky, 2004), Cowdery takes us through the expansive line of Beam distillers.*

It is hard to imagine another major American industry that has been as dominated by one family as the American whiskey industry has been by the Beams. No other family can compare to the Beams in sheer numbers, nor in the number of different companies affected. In part, this is because the clan is simply huge. Generation after generation, Beam families with 10 or more children have been common. In an industry that is so close knit and concentrated, it also isn't surprising that most of the other prominent families are connected to the Beams by marriage.

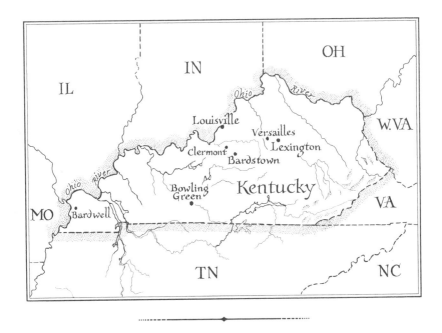

While members of the Beam family have owned a plant or two, they are most notable as the whiskey-making employees of others, including at the company that still bears the family name [although now owned by industry giant Brown-Forman]. And, they have not been limited to Kentucky. Everett Beam was master distiller at the Michter Distillery in Pennsylvania. Charlie Beam worked for Seagrams in Baltimore. Otis Beam worked at a distillery in Indiana. During Prohibition, Joe and Harry Beam operated a distillery in Mexico, while Guy Beam ran one in Canada.

All the whiskey-making Beams trace their lineage back to Johannes Jacob Beam, a Pennsylvanian of German descent who came to Kentucky by way of Maryland and, along the way, Americanized his

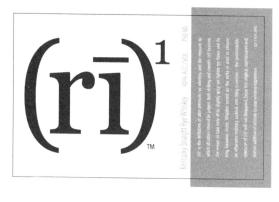

name to Jake Beam. He was a miller and distiller, a common combination in those days. Jacob and his wife, Mary, had 12 children. By 1795, they were in Kentucky and he was making whiskey alongside one of his sons, David. This is where the line splits, because this David Beam— who had 11 children—had three sons who made whiskey, as did many of their progeny. The three whiskey-makers were, in order of birth, Joseph B. Beam, David M. Beam and John H. "Jack" Beam.

The oldest and most prolific of the sons of David Beam was Joseph B., born in 1825. We don't know much about him except that he lived to be 91, he and his wife, Mary Ellen, had 14 children, and two of their sons became prominent whiskey-makers. We do know quite a bit about his two whiskey-making sons. The first was Minor Case Beam. (When you have 14 kids, at least one odd name is inevitable.) He worked at several places before buying an interest in the F. M. Head Distillery at Gethsemane, in southern Nelson County, Kentucky, which he eventually renamed the M.C. Beam Distillery.

In 1910, he sold out to J. B. Dant, who owned the distillery next door and wanted to use both plants to make his popular Yellowstone bourbon, which was named after the national park. Minor's son, Guy, worked at several Kentucky distilleries before and after Prohibition. During Prohibition he ran a Canadian distillery for the Wathen family's

American Medicinal Spirits Company, where he made Old Crow and Old Grand-Dad, presumably for surreptitious export back into the USA. Guy and his wife, Mary, had 10 children. One of their sons, Jack, worked at the Barton Distillery in Bardstown. Another son, Walter (known as Toddy), owned Bardstown's most popular liquor store, which is still called Toddy's today.

The other son of Joseph B. Beam who worked in the whiskey business was his namesake, Joseph L., who had a long career as a distiller and also produced seven distiller sons. If Joseph L. Beam and his "boys" had been the only Beams in the whiskey business, it still would be an amazing story.

Joe Beam's first distillery job, at age 14, was at his Uncle Jack's place, Early Times. At age 19, Joe became master distiller at his older brother's Gethsemane plant. After that he worked at several other distilleries, some simultaneously, including Tom Moore and Mattingly & Moore, which were both located where the Barton Distillery is today, and S.P. Pendergast, the notorious political boss of Kansas City. When Prohibition arrived, Joe was master distiller and part owner at F. G. Walker, whose president at the time was his cousin, Jim Beam.

Joe Beam's "boys," his seven distiller sons, were born between 1895 and 1910, so they mostly missed the pre-Prohibition industry. During Prohibition, Joe took his son Harry, who was still a child, with him to Juarez, Mexico, where he set up and ran a distillery for an old Kentucky whiskey concern, Waterfill & Frazier. They took apart the Kentucky plant, carted the pieces to Mexico, and reassembled it there.

Harry (full name Henry Milburn Beam), born in 1910, was the youngest of the seven brothers. The others, in birth order, were Joseph Elmo, known as Elmo, born 1895; Roy Marion, known as Roy, born 1898; Frederic Otis, known as Otis, born 1900; Wilmer Bernard, known as Wilmer, born 1903; Desmond Aloysius, known as Desmond, born 1905, and Charles Everett, known as Everett, born 1907.

By 1929, Joe and Harry had returned from Mexico, and Joe had won election as Nelson County's jailer. That December, Joe and Roy became the first distillers to legally make whiskey in the United States since the advent of Prohibition. Not only was the A. Ph. Stitzel plant in Louisville one of the few distilleries with a medicinal whiskey license, it was also one of the few with an operable distillery. In 1929, with medicinal stocks running low (and repeal looking increasingly probable), the federal government gave Stitzel permission to fire up its stills and, naturally, the Stitzel family called in the Beams to do the job.

David's middle son was his namesake, David M. Beam. Two of David's four sons also became distillers. The older of the two was James Beauregard "Jim" Beam, born in 1864, who would become the most famous Beam of them all.

Jim and his younger brother, Park, took over the family business in 1892, along with their sister's husband, Albert J. Hart. By this time, the distillery had a mashing capacity of 150 bushels of grain per day, and their four rackhouses could store up to 10,000 barrels of aging whiskey. They operated this distillery until Prohibition closed it. As Prohibition

approached, Jim also bought a controlling interest in the F. G. Walker plant where his cousin, Joe, was master distiller and a part-owner.

Jim Beam married Mary Catherine Montgomery in 1897. Uncharacteristically for the Beams, Jim and Mary Catherine had just three children: a son, T. Jeremiah, and two daughters, Mildred and Margaret. As soon as he was old enough (about 13), "Jerry" (they spelled it "Jere" but pronounced it "Jerry") went to work at the distillery. His sister, Margaret, married Frederick Booker Noe, and one of their sons, Booker Jr., went to work there, too. He would eventually oversee the Jim Beam Company distillery in Boston, Kentucky, and become world famous as the company's spokesperson, a role that is now being taken over by his son, Fred (formally Frederick Booker Noe III).

When Prohibition ended, Jim (age 70), Park (66) and their sons rounded up some investors and built a new distillery at the Clermont site. They resurrected the Old Tub brand, adding to it a new bourbon called simply "Jim Beam." Jere ran the business side, and Park's two sons, Carl (known as Shucks) and Earl, made the whiskey. Jim Beam retired in 1944 and died in 1947.

The Beams at Jim Beam and their cousins at Heaven Hill were always friendly competitors, regularly swapping equipment and parts, and helping each other whenever needed. At times, the two companies have deliberately bought the same equipment to make parts swaps easier. It has always been that way among the Beams.

So far as is known, all of the many Beams have been practical distillers, which means the yeast they use is propagated from a wild strain. The alternative is scientific distilling, in which a pure strain yeast bred in a laboratory and manufactured in a factory is used. With pure strain yeast, every spore is identical, and such yeasts can be manufactured in dry form. In contrast, wild yeast is also known as "jug yeast" because it must be kept in a liquid medium and constantly tended lest an undesirable strain take over and spoil it. A practical distiller will mix his special medium and then capture a suitable yeast from the air. This can be a very hit-or-miss proposition. Booker Noe often told the story of his grandfather "stinking up the house" while trying to propagate a suitable yeast at the end of Prohibition.

Of the Beam family members active in recent decades, the best known has been Booker Noe who died on February 24, 2004, at the age of 74. Booker started working at the distillery named for his grandfather in 1951 and rose to be master distiller at the company's second plant in Boston, Kentucky, a job he held for 32 years.

As master distiller, Booker was expected to monitor the bourbon aging in the company's rackhouses and was able to help himself to any whiskey that interested him in that vast network. He found that for his personal consumption, he favored bourbon from his plant that had been aged for between six and eight years. He took it straight from the barrel, at about 126 proof, usually running it into a 1.75 liter Jim Beam white label bottle to take home. Because it came straight from the barrel, the whiskey was not filtered, as most bourbon is prior to bottling. This was, literally, "Booker's Bourbon" long before there was a product by that name.

In 1987, Beam Company executives were looking for an unusual Christmas gift for their customers and suppliers. One of the executives had tasted Booker's private stock and suggested a special, limited bottling of Booker's special whiskey that would include a message from Booker. The gift was so successful wholesale customers virtually demanded that the company introduce it as a product, which they did the following year. This led to Booker's role as spokesperson for Booker's Bourbon and the three other super-premium bourbons Beam released as the Small Batch Collection. One of the others was a parallel personal bourbon that Booker's cousin, Baker Beam, selected from rackhouses at Clermont.

Naturally witty and likable, Booker was surprisingly good at public speaking and interview-giving. He had an unhurried, homespun style that perfectly suited the brand. After he retired from active distilling in 1992, Booker continued to be a globetrotting spokesperson for the company. His son, Fred, was gradually assuming that role as Booker's health declined and, with his father's death, he has become the company's sole link to its Beam heritage. An heir to that throne, Frederick Booker Noe IV, is already in the wings. Like any crown prince, the young gentleman has a job waiting for him whenever he wants it.

In most of America, the ancient tradition of passing a trade from parent to child has been lost, but it lives on in at least parts of the Beam family. As long as whiskey is made in America somewhere, somehow a Beam probably will be making it.

The
ORIGINAL SCOTCH *and* ITS HEIRS

CHARLES MacLEAN

Lost in the mists of Scotland are the origins of the country's indigenous whisky. But, what is known is that the original style made exclusively with malted barley by moonshiners and legal distillers alike took a sharp turn by the 1700s. In his seminal reference work **Whiskeypedia: A Gazetteer of Scotch Whisky,** *(Birlinn Ltd. of Edinburgh, Scotland, 2009), whisky historian and lecturer Charles MacLean explains the change of direction that led to the Scotch whiskies the world's consumers know today.*

Whisky made in Scotland from malted barley is the original Scotch, although by the late 18th Century, with the arrival of large-scale commercial distilling in the Lowlands, mixed grains (wheat and rye, as well as barley) were being used.

With the invention of the continuous still in the late 1820s—perfected and patented by Aeneas Coffey, former Inspector of Excise in Dublin, in 1830, Lowland distillers gradually came to devote themselves to grain whisky production in such stills, producing very pure, very high strength, somewhat bland spirit with which they inundated the new

industrial towns in the Central Belt of Scotland, as well as sending qualities to England for rectification into gin.

Pot still malt whisky was extremely variable in flavor. Like Longfellow's little girl, "When she was good, she was very, very good and when she was bad she was horrid!" It was drunk straight and young in the Highlands and mixed into a punch in the Lowlands, with water, sugar, lemons and sometimes spices. The first reference to the benefits of maturation that I know of is in Elizabeth Grant of Rothiemurchus's "Memoirs of a Highland Lady," where she recalls sending "pure Glenlivet whisky . . . long in the wood, long in uncorked bottles [This is mysterious!], mild as milk and with the real contraband *goût* [i.e., taste] in it" for the delectation of King George IV in Edinburgh in August 1822.

It is safe to suppose that wine and spirits merchants would have mixed the light grain whisky with variable and pungent malts to create a drink with broader appeal, from at least the 1820s. Many were familiar with blending teas, wines and cordials, which were often also part of their stock in trade. But, the first branded blend appeared in 1853, Usher's Old Vatted Glenlivet, and only after Gladstone's Spirits Act of 1860, which allowed the mixing of malt and grain whiskies under bond—i.e., before duty had to be paid—that blended Scotch took off.

And take off it did—in a very big way, helped by a variety of factors, not the least of which was the devastation of European vineyards by the louse *Phylloxera vastetrix*.

By the late 1860s, non-vintage cognac was unobtainable, and since brandy-and-soda was the drink of the English middle classes, this caused considerable dismay. Blended scotch (and soda) was not so improved as to be in a position to replace it.

Historians refer to the 1890s as the era of "The Whiskey Boom." Henceforward the fortunes of malt whisky distillers would be inextricably linked to those of the blenders, and the leading blending houses built or sought or took an interest in malt distilleries in order to secure the fillings for their blends. Thirty-three new distilleries were commissioned during the 1890s, 21 of them on Speyside—almost all of which are still in operation.

Alfred Barnard, the indefatigable Victorian traveller and editor of *Harper's* magazine, visited 188 malt distilleries in the late 1880s while compiling his monumental 1887 book *The Whisky Distilleries of The United Kingdom,* the first and still the most thorough account of distilling in these islands.

"'We shall be treading on delicate grounds when we refer to the fact that there are those who hold that the future of the Whisky trade lied with Malt Whisky.'"

With considerable foresight, he remarked: "We shall be treading on delicate grounds when we refer to the fact that there are those who hold that the future of the Whisky trade lied with Malt Whisky. Certainly 'the present' is not entirely in the hands of that product. Blenders without number can be found who will strenuously affirm that to give the public a moderate priced article with sufficient age, there is no way but to use good old Patent Still Grain Whisky as a basis."

[Now] never in history have so many varieties of malt whisky been available to the consumer. Never in history have there been so many enthusiasts for the drink! Demand has led to shortages of certain makes in certain markets, and to various ways of solving the problem. At its simplest, the price goes up. Or, the brand is pulled from specific markets to supply others. This happened to The Macallan in Taiwan in the early 21st Century where demand for the "traditional" style of sherried malt was met by moving stocks from other markets and replacing them with a parallel range of ages, matured in ex-bourbon casks, of which the company had plenty.

Famously, Diageo attempted to meet the demand for its Cardhu in Spain by introducing "Cardhu Pure Malt," a mix of Cardhu and Glendullan. The industry was outraged—or at least Diageo's competitors were, principally William Grant & Sons who raised a storm of protest, maintaining that consumers were being conned, and that the reputation of single malt Scotch would be tarnished. "Pure Malt" was withdrawn, and the Scotch Whisky Association set up a committee to look into definitions.

What is certain is that stocks of old mature whisky are in big demand, especially for deluxe and super deluxe labels, which are leading the way in the emergent markets. I have been assured by the larger distillery owners that supplies of malt for single bottling have been "ring fenced" and guaranteed, but we will see. Already, and in spite of what the independent bottlers were saying to me a year ago, good casks of mature whisky are becoming difficult to find. So it may be that our choice of malts will narrow, as independents leave the trade—or become distillers, as an increasing number are doing.

These are exciting times for Scotch!

The UNSETTLING of AMERICA

no. 3

Thousands of textbooks, nonfiction works, and novels have been written about the rough-and-ready life of the young United States of America.

From its earliest years as a British colony to the opening decades of its existence as an independent nation, the drinking habits of its populace played an immense role in commerce, legislation, and popular culture.

And, as we will see in the following essays, those drinking habits underwent tremendous changes that helped set American society apart from that of its various national antecedents.

FROM RUM *to* WHISKEY *in the* NEW U.S.A.

TOM STANDAGE

*Much of the "Triangle Trade" in the American Colonial
Period was centered on the cycle of dealing in rum, molasses,
and slaves, a practice so ingrained yet controversial that it
was the topic of a centerpiece song in the Broadway musical
1776 in which the actor portraying Edward Rutledge of
Virginia delivers it during the debates over the wording of
the Declaration of Independence. Molasses shipped from
the Caribbean was distilled into rum in New England and
Britain which in turn was traded for bodies in West Africa,
often bought from native tribal leaders who had conquered
them, to be shipped in chains to the Caribbean to work on
sugar cane plantations where molasses was produced—an
insidiously self-perpetuating set of undertakings, decried
even in their time while serving as the underpinnings of
global economies. But, after the American Revolution,
public tastes changed drastically, a change that, coupled
with the new nation's financial woes, eventually acted as a
catalyst for both the Whiskey Rebellion in Pennsylvania
and the development of the new state of Kentucky. The
English journalist and author Tom Standage chronicles these
developments in this excerpt from his book* A History of
the World in Six Glasses *(Walker Publishing Co., 2005).*

Rum was the drink of the Colonial Period and the American Revolution, but many of the citizens of the young nation soon turned their backs on it in favor of another distilled drink.

As settlers moved westward, away from the Eastern Seaboard, they switched to drinking whiskey, distilled from fermented cereal grains. One reason was that many of the settlers were of Scotch-Irish origin and had experience of grain distilling. The supply of molasses, from which rum was made, had also been disrupted during the war. And while grains such as barley, wheat, rye and corn were difficult to grow near the coast—hence the early colonists' initial difficulties with making beer—they could be cultivated more easily inland.

Rum, in contrast, was a maritime product, made in coastal towns from molasses imported by sea. Moving it inland was expensive. Whiskey could be made almost anywhere and did not depend on imported ingredients that could be taxed or blockaded.

By 1791 there were over five thousand pot stills in western Pennsylvania alone, one for every six people. Whiskey took on the duties that had previously been fulfilled by rum. It was a compact form of wealth: A packhorse could carry four bushels of grain, but it could carry twenty-four bushels that had been distilled into whiskey.

Whiskey was used as a rural currency, traded for other essentials such as salt, sugar, iron, powder and shot. It was given to farm workers, used in birth and death rituals, consumed whenever legal documents

were signed, given to jurors in courthouses and to voters by campaigning politicians. Even clergymen were paid in whiskey.

So, when the secretary of the U.S. Treasury, Alexander Hamilton, began to look for a way to raise money to pay off the vast national debt incurred during the Revolutionary War, imposing a federal excise duty on the production of distilled drinks seemed an obvious choice. The excise would raise money and might discourage people from drinking too much. Hamilton believed that such an excise would be "favourable to the agriculture, to the economy, to the morals, and to the health of the society."

In March 1791, a law was passed: From July 1, distillers could pay either an annual levy or an excise duty of at least seven cents on each gallon of liquor produced, depending on its strength. An immediate outcry arose, particularly along the western frontier. The excise seemed particularly unfair to the inland settlers because it applied to liquor as it left the still, not at the point of sale. This meant that whiskey produced for private consumption or barter was still subject to excise. Furthermore, many of the settlers had come to America to get away from revenue collectors and government interference. They complained that the new federal government was no better than the British government, whose rule America had just shaken off.

The disagreement over the whiskey excise also reflected the deeper divide over the balance of power between the state and the federal government. By and large, the inhabitants of the eastern territories were happier than those of the southern and western ones with the idea that federal law should take precedence over state law. The new law—which specified, among other things, that offenders would be tried in federal court in Philadelphia, rather than in local courts—seemed to favor eastern, federalist interests.

James Jackson of Georgia declared in the House of Representatives that the excise would "deprive the mass of the people of almost the only luxury they enjoy, that of distilled spirits." If it was not opposed, he asked, what might come next? "The time will come," Jackson warned, "when a shirt shall not be washed without an excise."

Once the new law came into force, many farmers refused to pay up. Revenue collectors were attacked, their documents stolen and destroyed, and the saddles taken from their horses and cut into pieces.

The opposition was strongest in the fiercely separatist western Pennsylvania frontier counties of Fayette, Allegheny, Westmoreland and Washington. Groups of farmers opposed to the excise began to coordinate organized resistance. Distillers who paid the excise had holes shot in their stills. Notices advocating disobedience appeared on trees. Congress amended

> *"The new law—which specified, among other things, that offenders would be tried in federal court in Philadelphia, rather than in local courts— seemed to favor eastern, federalist interests."*

the law in 1792 and 1794 to reduce the tax on rural distillers and gave the state courts jurisdiction to try offenders. But this failed to quell the opposition. Hamilton, who realized that the authority of the federal government was now at stake, sent federal marshals to western Pennsylvania to serve writs on several farmers who had refused to pay.

Violence flared after one such farmer, William Miller, was served with a writ in July 1794. A shot was fired at the marshal's party by one of Miller's associates, though no one was hurt. Over the next two days the two groups skirmished, the mob of armed "whiskey boys" opposed to the excise swelled to five hundred, and there were deaths on both sides.

David Bradford, an ambitious attorney, assumed leadership of the whiskey boys and called on the local people for support. Around six thousand men gathered at Braddock's Field, near Pittsburgh. Bradford was elected major general of this impromptu army. Amid high spirits, military exercises and target practice, the rebels passed resolutions advocating secession from the United States and the establishment of a new independent state.

Convinced by Hamilton that decisive action was necessary, President George Washington requisitioned thirteen thousand militiamen from eastern Pennsylvania, New Jersey, Virginia and Maryland. These troops, along with artillery pieces, baggage and supplies of tax-paid whiskey, were sent over the mountains to Pittsburgh to demonstrate the preeminence of the federal government to the secessionists. The nascent rebellion was, however, already crumbling. As the army approached, Bradford fled and his supporters melted away. Ironically, the arrival of the militia to take on the whiskey boys did much to resolve the problem: At the end of their march, the federal soldiers wanted more whiskey, which they paid for in hard cash.

This provided the distillers of western Pennsylvania the funds with which to pay the excise.

A token group of twenty rebels were taken back to Philadelphia and paraded through the streets. But, other than being held in jail for a few months, they escaped punishment. Two of their number were sentenced to death but were pardoned by the president.

Ultimately, the liquor excise failed and was repealed a few years later. Paying the federal militia to suppress the rebellion cost $1.5 million, nearly one-third of the entire excise duties collected during the ten years the excise law was in force. But, while both the rebellion and the excise failed, the suppression of the Whiskey Rebellion, the first tax protest to take place since independence, forcefully illustrated that federal law could not be ignored and was a defining moment in the early history of the United States.

The failure of the rebellion also led to the development of another drink, as Scotch-Irish rebels moved farther west into the new state of Kentucky. There they began to make whiskey from corn as well as rye. The production of this new kind of whiskey was pioneered in Bourbon County, so that the drink became known as bourbon. The use of corn, an indigenous crop, gave it a unique flavor.

In the last years of his life, George Washington himself established a whiskey distillery. The idea came from his farm manager, a Scot who suggested that the grains produced at Washington's estate, Mount

Vernon, could be profitably made into whiskey. Two stills began operating in 1797, and at the peak of production, shortly before Washington's death in December 1799, there were five stills. That year he produced eleven thousand gallons of rye, which he sold locally, making a profit of $7,500. He also gave barrels of it to family and friends. "Two hundred gallons of Whiskey will be ready this day for your call," Washington wrote to his nephew on October 29, 1799, "and the sooner it is taken the better, as the demand (in these parts) is brisk."

Washington's activities as a whiskey maker presented a stark contrast to the attitudes of another of America's founding fathers, Thomas Jefferson. He denounced "the poison of whiskey" and famously remarked that "no nation is drunken where wine is cheap, and none sober where the dearness of wine substitutes ardent spirits as the common beverage."

Jefferson did his best to cultivate vines in America and advocated a reduction in the excise duty charged on imported wine as "the only antidote to the bane of whiskey." But his cause was hopeless. Wine was far more expensive, contained less alcohol and lacked the American connotations of whiskey, an unpretentious drink associated with independence and self-sufficiency.

GRANT, BABCOCK,
– *and the* –
WHISKEY RING

TIMOTHY RIVES

American presidents and spirits are no strangers to each other. George Washington was the young nation's largest distiller. Franklin D. Roosevelt publicly made what was called, perhaps whimsically, the nation's first legal cocktail after the repeal of Prohibition. Harry Truman was a noted bourbon enthusiast. But, in between Washington and those latter-day worthies came one Ulysses S. Grant, Civil War hero and eighteenth U.S. president. He was involved in a variety of scandals during his administration, as have been other presidents. However, he was the only one for whom whiskey was at the center of an upheaval. In this Fall 2000 article for the magazine Prologue: Quarterly of the National Archives and Records Administration, *archives specialist Timothy Rives details what went on.*

"I always knew when I was in trouble that Grant was thinking about me and would get me out. And he did."

–Gen. William Tecumseh Sherman

Bound with "hooks of steel." That's how Maj. Gen. Greenville M. Dodge described Ulysses S. Grant's loyalty to his country, his God, and his friends. The same loyalty that pulled Grant, who had fought in the Mexican War in the 1840s, back to active army service in 1861 to win the Civil War called him in 1868 to the presidency to win the peace.

"I have been forced into it in spite of myself," he complained to his friend, Gen. William Tecumseh Sherman. But the Savior of the Union feared that the blood-bought gains of the Civil War were threatened by the depredations of the "mere trading politicians" whom he now felt duty bound to defeat. So he ran and won on a platform constructed largely on his moral authority as the Hero of Appomattox.

In his inaugural address, Grant pledged to be a "purely administrative officer" who would "have a policy to recommend but none"—he asserted in pointed contrast to President Andrew Johnson— "to enforce against the will of the people." Grant proposed laws to ensure "the security of person, property, and free religious and political opinion in our common country." He advocated hard money policies "to protect the national honor"—and his rich friends, critics then and now charge. . . . All in all, Grant promised peace, prosperity, and progress. But that was not to be his legacy of his White House years.

In December 1875, a grand jury in St. Louis indicted Gen. Orville E. Babcock who, as the private secretary of the President of the United States, his friend and patron Grant, was one of the most powerful and influential persons in the federal government. He was charged with conspiracy to defraud the Treasury of the United States.

Babcock's indictment as one of the "Whiskey Ring" co-conspirators and his protestation of innocence would inspire Grant to take unprecedented executive action in defense of a man who had been one of his closest associates since the Civil War. And the indictment and subsequent trial would cause the greatest "national excitement" since the fall of Richmond in the war more than a decade earlier. The President, against almost everyone's advice, would make a mark in history that has yet to be matched.

This is the story of how far Grant went—and how much further he almost went—to defend his good friend Babcock against criminal charges. It is drawn from long-overlooked records in the holdings of the National Archives and Records Administration in Kansas City, the accounts of contemporary trial observers, and the work of other historians of the Grant administration.

Grant's White House years coincided with a period of painful change and transition in the country. The South resisted Reconstruction; the rest of the country resisted nothing. Turning from war to peace with a vengeance, Americans busied themselves conquering the western territories, laying great webs of railroad, forming powerful combinations of capital, and manufacturing an unprecedented number of goods. It was a sumptuous and acquisitive age.

Historian Vernon Parrington likened

"Babcock's indictment as one of the 'Whiskey Ring' co-conspirators and his protestation of innocence would inspire Grant to take unprecedented executive action in defense of a man who had been one of his closest associates since the Civil War."

its patronage politics and "come and get it" morality to a "Great Barbeque."

"It was sound Gilded Age doctrine," he wrote. "To a frontier people what was more democratic than a Barbeque, and to a paternalistic age what was more fitting than that the state should provide the beeves for roasting. Let all come and help themselves. As a result the feast was Gargantuan in its rough plenty."

Friends, family, and officials of the Grant administration embodied this corpulent spirit conspicuously, attracting charges of financial and political corruption unrivaled perhaps until recent times. Its many scandals are well known: the Gold Conspiracy, Santo Domingo, the Sanborn Contract, to name but a few. Grant, incorruptible but politically naïve, largely escapes blame for the failings of his subordinates, many of whom were investigated at one time or another. A man with uxorious-like devotion to his friends, Grant often failed to see the worst in his associates, even when it was laid before his eyes. Grant's offense is ignorance at best, pettifoggery at worst. Grant's great private virtue—loyalty—could be a public vice when proffered liberally.

The various Grant scandals had little in common except for the hand of the ubiquitous Babcock. "The eternal cabal—with Babcock always at the centre!" wrote one despairing historian of the administration. Born in 1835 in Franklin, Vermont, Babcock joined Grant's staff at Vicksburg, two years after graduating West Point. By war's end, he wore a brevet star and had joined Grant's circle for good. It was Babcock who was waiting for Grant with Confederate Gen. Robert E. Lee at the Appomattox courthouse in 1865 so Lee could surrender to Grant and end the Civil War. When Grant entered the White House four years later, Babcock followed.

Fighting scandal was practically a state of being in the Grant White House, but the Whiskey Ring indictment was trouble, perhaps the worst the President—and certainly Babcock—had seen since the war.

Republican party operatives formed the Whiskey Ring in 1871 to raise funds for political campaigns in Missouri and other western states. Liberal Republicans, led by Grant foe Senator Carl Schurz, had conquered the Missouri state party, putting Grant's 1872 reelection plans in jeopardy. Once an admirer of the President, Schurz—a former German revolutionary, Union Army general, and journalist—had grown disappointed with Grant. By early 1871, he was in open rebellion and stated confidently that the "superstition that Grant is the necessary man is rapidly giving way. The spell is broken, and we have only to push through to the breach."

To keep the Schurz forces in check, Grant sent an ally, Supervisor of Internal Revenue Gen. John McDonald, to hold Missouri Republicans in his camp. "Soon," wrote historian William Hesseltine, "[McDonald] was unearthing a new source of revenue for Republican campaigns." Illicit whiskey money began to fill campaign stores and finance partisan newspapers to print articles favorable to the Grant administration.

Complex in detail, but simple in design, the ring made money by selling more whiskey than it reported to the Treasury Department. Its success required collusion at every point of the production, distribution, and taxation process.

To pull it off, ringleaders recruited, impressed, and blackmailed distillers, rectifiers, gaugers, storekeepers, revenue agents, and Treasury clerks into the operation. They split the 75-cents-a-gallon tax money they had stolen a number of ways. U.S. Attorney David P. Dyer, the man who one day would prosecute the whiskey thieves, later explained the arrangements of the ring to congressional investigators:

"They kept an account at the distillers of all the illicit whisky that was made, and the gaugers and store-keepers were paid from one to two dollars for each barrel that was turned out . . . and every Saturday reported to the collector of the ring the amount of crooked whisky, and either the distiller or the gauger paid the money over as the case might be. The arrangement between distiller and rectifier was that 35 cents . . . was divided between him and the rectifier. That division was made by the distiller selling crooked whisky . . . at 17 cents a gallon less than the market price. That is how the rectifier got his share of the amount retained by the distiller. The amount paid to the officers was on each Saturday evening taken to the office of the supervisor of internal revenue and there divided . . . and distributed among them."

"'They kept an account at the distillers of all the illicit whisky that was made, and the gaugers and store-keepers were paid from one to two dollars for each barrel that was turned out . . .'"

From November 1871 to November 1872, the five principal members of the Ring received between $45,000 and $60,000 each. Four participating distilleries received the same amount. It was a profitable venture. . . . The ring survived its humble slush fund origins to become by 1873 a purely criminal enterprise, defrauding the federal Treasury of an estimated million and a half dollars a year. It operated as long as Treasury Department officials ignored it. The thievery might have continued had Grant not appointed Benjamin H. Bristow secretary of the Treasury in June 1874. . . . Rings for the scheme operated in a number of different cities. Bristow made the destruction of the rings his personal and political crusade, but early efforts to unravel the corruption failed. . . .

On January 26, 1875, in an attempt to end the fraud, Bristow ordered the transfer of Internal Revenue supervisors, an act he believed would catch crooked officers off guard and uncover their misdeeds. Grant initially supported the order but forced its suspension within a week. Grant opposed the transfers because, he reasoned, it gave the crooked distillers and agents too much time to redress their accounts and erase evidence of fraud. Furthermore, it would remove trusted political allies like the able McDonald. . . . Bristow blamed Grant's change of mind on high-level interference. . . . Frustrated with the course of his department's investigation and the revoked transfer order, Bristow welcomed the offer of private assistance. *St. Louis Democrat* commercial editor and Cotton Exchange secretary Myron Colony became Bristow's secret investigator in early March of 1875.

Well known in St. Louis business circles, Colony was a familiar, innocuous presence who routinely collected business information and statistics. The local business community was used to seeing Colony ask questions and write things down as the *Democrat's* commercial editor, so his "investigation" did not arouse any suspicions.

He and his small group of spies began recording the quantity of grain arriving at each distillery, the amount of liquor arriving at the rectifiers, as well as illegal night distilling. Colony compared the records of the distillers and rectifiers with what he and his men had seen, what the producers and refiners reported, and what the shipping and tax records revealed. The discrepancies showed the fraud in bright relief.

In just four weeks, Colony and his men had collected the information Bristow needed to arrest the whiskey thieves.

Armed with the reports from Colony and other informers in principal distilling cities across the country, Bristow struck in May 1875. Federal lawmen arrested more than 300 ring members and seized distilleries and rectifiers. U.S. Marshals in St. Louis arrested, among many others, Supervisor McDonald, Revenue Agent John A. Joyce, and Collector Constantine Maguire, as well as [*St. Louis Democrat* editor William Meade] Fishback's competitor, William McKee, proprietor of the rival *St. Louis Globe*. Bristow had finally exposed the St. Louis Whiskey Ring. . . .

Would Babcock prove to be the "high-level" interloper whom Bristow suspected to be meddling behind the scenes in Washington? Would his exposure of the insider be enough to carry Bristow to the White House in the 1876 election?

The law, in the form of Bristow, was now at Grant's door, poised to apprehend the President's closest and most trusted aide—if not the President himself.

A grand jury examined the evidence throughout the summer of 1875. Indictments of the "very worst of them"—including McDonald and Joyce—came in June. U.S. attorneys found cryptic telegrams traced to Babcock, which indicated his role in obstructing the early Bristow investigations. "I succeeded. They will not go. I will write you. Sylph," read one particularly suspicious dispatch. But Babcock remained free, at least for the time being.

In July, Attorney General Edward Pierrepont and Secretary Fish traveled to Grant's summer home in Long Branch, NJ, to discuss the evidence that linked Babcock to the scandal. Despite his affection for and confidence in his aide, Grant endorsed the work of the grand jury: "Let no guilty man escape if it can be avoided."

By August, however, as the evidence drifted higher and higher around Babcock, Grant's attitude toward the investigation changed from overt approval to tacit disapproval.

Confronted with the incriminating telegrams, Babcock denied wrongdoing. Grant believed him and even corroborated his absurd and risible explanation that the telegram in question referred to a past event that had not yet occurred at the time that Babcock wrote the message.

"Friends and advisers encouraged the President to believe the worst about the political ambitions of Bristow ..."

If the trail led to Babcock, it entered the White House. Friends and advisers encouraged the President to believe the worst about the political ambitions of Bristow and the political agenda of the Whiskey Ring prosecutors. Grant's St. Louis associates also warned him that his enemies would not stop until they indicted the entire administration. "Grant," wrote one historian, "quickly imbibed these suspicions." Alarmed, he assigned C. S. Bell, a former postal department special agent, to spy on the government prosecutors. Back in St. Louis, jurors convicted McDonald and Joyce. The court sentenced them to three years in the state penitentiary, and fined them thousands of dollars.

Meanwhile, the grand jury moved closer to Babcock.

The political battle simmering beneath the surface of the Whiskey Ring trials intensified with the conviction of W. O. Avery, the former chief clerk of the Treasury Department. In his closing argument, prosecutor John B. Henderson, a former U.S. senator from Missouri who had voted to acquit President Andrew Johnson, accused Babcock of obstructing justice. More important, he attacked Grant when he likened the position of a minor Treasury official allegedly pressured by Babcock and the President to call off his investigation of whiskey fraud to that of a slave. Attorney General Pierrepont fired the impolitic Henderson without pay. . . .

"At Grant's command, Attorney General Pierrepont issued an order to prosecutors forbidding them to grant immunity to convicted criminals who turned state's evidence."

On December 9, 1875, the grand jury issued the dreaded indictment largely on the basis of the "Sylph" telegram. The court set his trial for February 7, 1876. . . . At Grant's command, Attorney General Pierrepont issued an order to prosecutors forbidding them to grant immunity to convicted criminals who turned state's evidence. . . . Secretary Fish feared that the President had undermined his own prosecutors' case on behalf of his aide, an ethically questionable if technically legal act. . . .

The case . . . hinged on the interpretation of telegrams alleged to have passed between General Babcock and the St. Louis conspirators, chiefly Supervisor of Internal Revenue McDonald and Revenue Agent Joyce. The correspondence began, prosecutors charged, at the death of Revenue Collector Charles W. Ford and the ring's effort to fill the vacancy with a man agreeable to the confines and rewards of their scheme.

The government accused Babcock of alerting Joyce to the arrival of

Treasury Department investigators in the spring of 1874 in order to give him time to fix affairs in St. Louis. Prosecutors alleged that this sort of advice flowed copiously from Babcock to Joyce and McDonald over the course of the Bristow investigations, culminating with the now-famous December 13, 1874, dispatch heralding Babcock's triumph over the Treasury inspectors: "I succeeded. They will not go. I will write you. Sylph."

The New York Times would later describe this message as Babcock's "crowning blunder." Additionally, the government presented this telegram, sent from Joyce to Babcock following the cancellation of the supervisor transfer order: "We have official information that the enemy weakens. Push things. Sylph." . . .

Grant knew the day would come when Babcock would have to face the charges against him in court, but the reality of that first day's proceedings both angered and moved the President to take unprecedented executive action.

He called a special cabinet meeting where he bitterly denounced the Babcock prosecution as being "aimed at himself." They are putting me on trial, Grant told his lieutenants. They already "had taken from him his secretaries and clerks, his messengers and doorkeepers," Hamilton Fish recorded in his diary. Now they threatened to take his beloved private secretary, the man who had been at his side at Vicksburg, at Appomattox, through the dark years of the Johnson administration, and the highs and lows of two rough terms in the White House. . . . Babcock is innocent, the President insisted. Of this, he said, he was as "confident as he lived."

Next, Grant, a man with a flair for the successful desperate measure, took one. He would testify for Babcock, he told his cabinet. He would get him out of trouble.

And he did.

A sitting President had never before—and has not since—testified voluntarily as a defense witness in a criminal trial. For Grant to do so, in person no less, was more than his Cabinet would bear. Secretary Fish warned Grant that "should the President go [to St. Louis], it would be a voluntary offering of himself as a witness for the defense in a criminal prosecution instituted by the government, of which the President is the representative and embodiment; that it would therefore place him in the attitude of volunteering as a witness to defeat the prosecution, which the law made it his duty to enforce."

Fish prevailed, to a point. Grant would testify for Babcock, but there would be no trip to St. Louis, no crowds in the street, no dramatic courtroom entrance—just a deposition taken in the quiet, controllable confines of the White House. . . . Judge Dillon instructed the jury that "evidence of persons of good character has more scope than in cases where the proof of offense is positive and direct." Conversely, "the testimony of conspirators is always to be received with extreme caution and weighed and scrutinized with great care by the jury, who should not rely upon it unsupported unless it produced in their minds, the fullest and most positive conviction of its truth."

Circumstantial evidence made up the case against Babcock. The message to the jury was clear: Believe Grant. Two hours after receiving their instructions, the "plain, honest, farmer-looking" members of the jury reentered the courtroom where they delivered a verdict of "not guilty."

The jurors then proceeded to the Lindell Hotel, where along with General Sherman and other dignitaries, they celebrated Babcock's acquittal and serenaded him with song.

Although Babcock won the battle, he lost the war.

Forced from Grant's side by cabinet officers concerned with

the propriety of his presence in the White House following the controversial trial, Babcock was indicted just 10 days later for his alleged role in yet another administration-related scandal, the Safe Burglary Conspiracy. Acquitted once more, he was appointed Chief Inspector of Lighthouses by the doggedly faithful Grant. In 1884, Babcock drowned near the coast of Mosquito Inlet, FL, in the line of duty. . . .

Although Grant's place in history as a Civil War general remains prominent and favorable—the hero of Appomattox who humbled Lee—his presidency is remembered most for the scandals created by the friends to whom he was so faithful and loyal.

The GREAT EXPERIMENT

no. 4

Much has been written by many people about the Volstead Act, the enabling legislation behind the Eighteenth Amendment to the U.S. Constitution known more commonly—and descriptively—as Prohibition; an era also known as "The Great Experiment."

From romantic tales of dancing and illicit drinking in speakeasies to stirring yarns of machine gun–wielding bootleggers to backwoods stills and overworked lawmen trying to keep things in line—think *The Untouchables*—we have had nearly a century of such literature that has sustained an entire sector of the entertainment industry.

But, some of the smaller writings have just as much drama and accurate insights as their better-known brethren, reducing a nationwide period of frenzy and confusion into sharply etched local vignettes.

THE MAN
in the OVERCOAT

DR. HARRY STEGMAIER

Herman J. Miller was a lifelong resident of Cumberland, located in mountainous western Maryland less than fifty miles from the presidential retreat at Camp David. He served on the city's Advisory Commission on Historical Matters and the Historic Preservation Commission during the 1970s. He was a member of the Cumberland Fire Department until his retirement. In 1978, he was the subject of an oral history by Dr. Harry Stegmaier of the history department at Frostburg State University in Maryland. The resulting text was entitled **Cumberland, Maryland, through the Eyes of Herman J. Miller.**

During the 1920s and early 1930s, so many arrests and convictions were made by dry agents that the Allegany County Jail could not hold all of the prisoners, so some were housed in the Garrett County Jail at Oakland, Maryland.

One bootlegger on North Mechanic Street had a box-like platform built out of a second story window over Wills Creek. If a raid should occur, the operator would just pull a rope and the bottom would drop out and the contents would drop down to the rocks below, for this is where he kept his whiskey. When the glass bottles hit the rocks, the bottles would shatter, and thus, no evidence.

A cheap, homemade still

One bootlegger I knew wore an overcoat all the time. People who didn't know him thought he was an eccentric, but he had a half-dozen pockets inside the coat in which he carried his stock of whiskey for sale.

One of the favorite places for good moonshine, to the ones in the know, was a well-known Liberty Street shop. Most speakeasies were ones that you got in, if they knew you, got your drink, and got out. Some were fixed up like club rooms, with chairs, tables, and some with slot machines.

People referred to the quality of liquor bought in the prohibition era, calling two dollar whiskey "Long Life" and the one dollar whiskey "Early Grave." While some bootleggers sold only whiskey, mostly their places sold both whiskey and home brew. Most fraternal clubs were for members only, but had both whiskey and beer for sale.

Some speakeasies stole the idea from the strictly private clubs and had membership cards made for the patrons of their places. As an example of how many wanted to sell liquor when the country went dry, there were thirty-six licenses issued for 1921 for soft drink establishments. Not all sold liquor, but most did. Some bootleggers would deliver to your home. You would use a code over the telephone. If you wanted three pints, you would ask for three pounds.

" Some bootleggers would deliver to your home. You would use a code over the telephone. If you wanted three pints, you would ask for three pounds."

On April 7, 1933, 3.2 beer [only 3.2% alcohol by volume, sometimes referred to as "near beer"] became legal. Baltimore, Hagerstown, and other parts of the state were selling the brew. Cumberland and Allegany Counties could not because a bill that had been passed in the General Assembly pertaining to county beer licenses stipulated that the applications became available on the day beer came back, but permits became effective only seven days later. You could buy beer on the first day of repeal in Pennsylvania. A store just over the state line on the Bedford Road was selling beer on the first day. A steady stream of Cumberlanders took advantage of the beer sale.

On Friday, April 14, 1933, beer could be bought in Allegany County. Those who could sell beer reported a good business. There were almost as many women as men customers.

With the return of beer, many speakeasies came out in the open, applied for licenses, and operated under regulations. It is worth noting that it has been only about two years since beer and liquor could be sold legally on Sunday in Allegany County. Many people of the area would go to [nearby] Ridgeley, West Virginia, to buy beer on Sundays. . . .

When it was all over and the country was again wet, there seemed to be no attachment of lawlessness or the stigma of hoodlum attached to the convicted bootleggers who had served time in jail. Some, in later years, joined highly regarded fraternal orders. Others operated successful businesses. William Harvey, who was considered to be the outstanding prohibition enforcement officer in Allegany County, became sheriff of Allegany County for a time.

AL CAPONE

The
CASE *of* CAPONE'S WHISKEY

JIM LEGGETT

There is perhaps no more enduring name, for good or for bad, from the Prohibition era than that of Chicago gangster Al Capone. He was a regular visitor to Detroit and, right across the Detroit River, to Windsor, Ontario, an area that was a hotbed of illicit activity at that time when alcohol was illegal in the United States but legal in Canada. Journalist Jim Leggett visited with a salvage diver who had located a cache of prize Scotch whisky from that period. (This article originally was published in **Whisky Magazine***, issue 50, Norfolk, England.)*

Dazzling sun shafts pierced the gloom where, 20 feet below the surface of the Detroit River, diver Leon Sehoyan groped his way towards a pile of grimy gunwales. Pursuing his summer weekend hobby of searching out old bottles he swam toward the wreck.

"I'd found hundreds of bottles in the river over the years, old beer, soda, even glass baby bottles, but nothing like this." Leon recalled how he'd stumbled upon a genuine rumrunner's booze boat.

Hardly recognizable in the mud, the old hull and her rusted engine piques Leon's excitement.

"Right away I suspected I'd found a Prohibition era rumrunner. When next I saw a couple wooden boxes still sealed and full of very old Scotch whisky, I knew I'd found a mother lode.

"Visions of high speed chases, revenue agents in hot pursuit, shooting wildly trying to stop this boat popped into my mind. I imagined ghosts of Al Capone, Elliot Ness and clandestine smuggling as I explored the wreck. Then I brushed silt away on one box; writing on the box, a British Royal seal and the legend: Alexander & MacDonald Leith NB Purveyors to the House of Lords.

"'I imagined ghosts of Al Capone, Elliot Ness and clandestine smuggling as I explored the wreck.'"

"I figured I'd come across a treasure stash of bootleg Scotch. Cases of the precious stuff were scattered near the wreck. I wrestled a case up to the surface, hoisted it aboard my boat then pried off the lid. A dozen dark green bottles glinted in sunlight for this first time in 80-odd years."

No whisky connoisseur will ever turn down the chance to sample a rare Scotch, even if it's been languishing like buried liquid treasure at the bottom of the Detroit River for decades. So rare were Leon's discoveries that even the most experienced whisky expert refused to venture a price for 100-year-old pot still malts. This precious golden potable was destined to cast new light on American bootlegging history.

Soon, Leon's mates were swapping tales of how their grandpas flaunted American law and made big bucks smuggling booze, of speedboat chases and waterfront shootouts.

Happily, news of the amazing find was confined to trusted pals, none of whom squealed as the secret stash headed gently for his cellar.

Fast forward.

"A few years later I picked up the newspaper, a story saying salvagers had just found that same wreck, plus an empty beer keg or two caught my eye."

"Bootlegger's boat to rise from Detroit River" reported the discovery of a 23-foot wooden runabout powered by a four-cylinder engine.

"Diver's plunge into the past, raise rumrunner's treasure" surmised the boat was used by rumrunners smuggling hooch into the United States from Canada.

"What they didn't find was her cargo of Prohibition-era whisky," Leon said. "I had to laugh reading that yarn. I'd gotten there first."

Leon scrawled on the margin of the two newspaper clippings— "The reason they only got empty bottles is because I got the full ones," and "This is the rum runner I got your Scotch off of. P.S. I'll show some of the others next time we have a drink."

I first met Leon while in Detroit on a news assignment, and immediately he heard my Glasgow accent; his eyes lit up as he confided he had something exciting to show me. Down in his cellar he pulled a dust cloth from a stack of boxes, reached into one and grabbed a bottle of Scotch.

JOHNNIE WALKER

Red Label

OLD SCOTCH WHISKY

DISTILLED, BLENDED AND BOTTLED IN SCOTLAND

Removing a neck foil, he twisted the cork, then poured us both a generous dram. 1905 was stamped on the seal.

"This whisky was destined for one of Capone's speakeasies," he said. "Now we have it. Cheers!"

Its big sleep at the bottom of the river hadn't diminished the taste of this vintage Sandy Mac, so we poured another wee nip as Leon agreed to take me downriver next day, to show me where his treasure was found. We left the Grosse Point (Michigan) Marina aboard Leon's 26-foot craft and headed south; 20 minutes later he throttled back, swooshed to a stop and dropped anchor. Donning his red wetsuit and mask, he beamed mischievously, then plopped backwards into the water. In minutes he was back, clutching a bottle in each hand.

"'I've found single bottles plus a couple of cases hereabouts, some dating from 1905, 1910 and the like ...'"

"I've found single bottles plus a couple of cases hereabouts, some dating from 1905, 1910 and the like," he said. "Their metallic cork seals preserve the stuff in perfect condition."

Sandy Mac, so the case wording read, had won "Gold Medals International" and "Highest Awards Exhibitor," followed by the embossed signature "Alexander Macdonald Ltd., Leith, Scotland."

Apart from minor water damage to some labels, the newfound bottles of old Scotch drying on the deck looked almost new.

"I'd never heard of Sandy Mac before finding this lot," he exclaimed.

Also found were single bottles of Johnny Walker, Old Smuggler and Gordon's Gin with flip-top caps. Some bottles carried the Royal Warrant "By Appointment to His Majesty the King."

By profession Leon is a barber. His chic hairstyling boutique in Grosse Pointe caters to the likes of the actress Sherylyn ("Twin Peaks") Fenn's family, including her famous rock star aunt, Suzi Quatro. Part-time he's a volunteer rescue diver with the Grosse Point Marine Rescue Unit. He's credited with saving several lives, too.

"I live near the water, so the cops often call me for help with submerged vehicles," he said.

The clandestine sport of bootlegging flourished in the Detroit area for about 14 years during Prohibition, and allegedly became the biggest employer and revenue maker next to the automobile industry.

In 1927, the U.S. government decided to make a big push to control the illicit liquor business in Detroit, and 100 or more handpicked Customs Service and Border Patrol officers joined others from the Prohibition Bureau to combat the smugglers.

Soon this giant posse was zooming all over the lakes and rivers in fast patrol boats trying to stem the flow of liquid gold that washed ashore, concealed in everything from phony eggshells to fake gas tanks.

But, the interdiction campaign was declared a flat failure after it was revealed in records from the Ontario Provincial Government that boats carrying some 3,388,016 gallons of liquor had left Windsor for

Detroit that year alone and U.S. Prohibition agents had managed to seize a mere teaspoonful—a paltry 148,211 gallons.

Leon's sunken boat wreck was probably one that almost was snared. Painted red, she carried a faded number on her side, and her bottom was blown away.

"When chased by Revenue agents, they'd take a shotgun, blow a hole in the boat and sink their cargo." Leon explained. "Later, when the coast was clear, they'd go back with grappling hooks to retrieve the booze; 500, maybe 1,000 cases were typical of loads carried aboard.

Ironically, it was Prohibition that led to the popularity of Scotch whisky in North America, during which genuine Scotch was prized above rubies. Home-brewed concoctions such as Black Strap, Panther Whisky, Happy Sally, Yack-Yack and the like often was lethal, causing blindness and even death among unsuspecting drinkers.

Canny Scots were quick to see an opportunity for fast money. Soon they were shipping their healthier products to Canada and the Caribbean. Schooners would sail openly just beyond the 12-mile limit, offloading their cargoes to speedboats sent out by American bootleggers to meet them.

According to a book on the legends of the Prohibition era, Bill McCoy from Florida was said to have made a million dollars, also landing himself a place in the dictionary. A gentleman of high principle, McCoy refused to carry any but the finest brands, so the expression "The real McCoy" became part of the English language.

Sampling wee nips from an old bottle one evening Leon wondered aloud what to do with his liquid treasure. The stuff was gathering dust beneath a faded British flag, and probably would still be there today had chance, opportunity and some swashbuckling daring not conspired to intervene.

His collection includes some picturesque names: Old Nobility Southern Sunshine, Gooderman Worts, Canadian Rye, Old Smuggler (dated 1910), Rum Clement and Havana Club Brand, and Canadian Club.

Since he'd decided to get rid of his collection, I offered to take a few bottles. As for the rest, whisky auctions are held regularly in Glasgow. I suggested he get in touch with Christie's; they might be interested in this unique stash.

"Yeah" he mused. "How fitting to return this grand old Scotch to its native land."

After an affirmative reply from Christie's, Leon decided to ship the whisky from Detroit to Glasgow as freight aboard a regular airline, only to run into red tape. Cargo officers said they wouldn't accept whisky. Disappointed, he rang me that night saying the deal was off. I suggested he try another ploy: Why not declare them antique bottles?

The plot worked and next day the re-named Scotch was speeding home again to Scotland. As auction day rolled around, Christie's sumptuous 50-page catalogue ran a fine black-and-white photograph showing off four of Leon's bottles: Lot 249—Old Nobility, Lot 250—Old Smuggler, Lot 251-2—Sandy MacDonald, showing front label and rear labels.

Lot 249 was described as Old Nobility Southern Sunshine, early 20th Century. Made and bottled by United Brands of Detroit,

Michigan. Stopper cork, paper tax seal. Glass embossed "Federal law forbids sale or re-use of this bottle." Level: low-shoulder. 100 proof. According to the catalogue it was expected to fetch between £150– 250 ($286–475).

As for Lot 251-2—Sandy Mac, the listing read: "A case of 'Sandy Mac' from an American cellar." There followed an in-depth description of the real Sandy MacDonald—early 20th Century, and 10 lines of glowing product promotional information, also noting "As supplied to the House of Lords."

Leon's collection of whisky created great interest among bidders in Glasgow. Adding to local mystique, a story about his remarkable find ran in Scotland's *Sunday Mail.* His Detroit finds were compared with the movie *Whisky Galore,* the comical true life yarn about the S.S. Politician which sank with thousands of cases of whisky off a Scottish island during World War II.

"I often wonder if the lucky folks who bid on Lot 251, my 100-year-old bottles of Scotch, ever realized they'd won themselves a tangible piece of America's and Al Capone's history," Leon mused while scrutinizing navigational maps, trying to figure where next to dive in search of lost liquid gold.

MOONSHINE
~ and the ~
MORNING GLASS

SCOTT WHEELER

Big cities and southern towns are among the best known locales for Prohibition activity stories. But bucolic Vermont, snug up against the Canadian border, had some of the more active home moonshiners and liquor smugglers of the era, not entirely unexpected since the area known as the Northeast Kingdom was sparsely populated, the border relatively unguarded, and alcohol was legal and readily available in Canada. Scott Wheeler, a prominent Vermont journalist and historian, tells in his book Rumrunners and Revenuers: Prohibition in Vermont *(New England Press Inc., 2002) the stories of fourteen different people and their experiences during the Great Experiment. This is one of them.*

Ten pounds of corn, ten pounds of sugar, and ten pounds of yeast, all placed in a 10-gallon milk can partially filled with water. That's about all it took to get the mash going," said Anatole Duquette of Barton, Vermont, as he recalled the first step in his family's moonshining. "Sometimes my mother would throw a few prunes into the mixture, perhaps for a little extra flavor.

"It was simple," Duquette said. "Anybody could make a batch of moonshine, and many people did."

Duquette, now in his early nineties, said that making their own liquor was just part of keeping a family tradition alive.

"We were just providing my father with his morning glass of whiskey. This was a ritual he began back in Quebec long before Prohibition. It was also part of the culture; many other French-Canadian immigrants had the same way of starting the day.

"We never thought of moonshining as breaking the law: no, we were law-abiding folks . . . and still are. In fact, my brother's boy, J. Paul Duquette, is the chief of police in Newport, Vermont," Duquette proudly pointed out.

"We were just providing my father with his morning glass of whiskey. This was a ritual he began back in Quebec long before Prohibition."

The family didn't abuse the alcohol they made, and only family and visiting relatives from Quebec drank it, even though his immigrant family could have used the money as they tried to sweat out a living as farmers. Duquette's father also refused to allow smugglers to hide their rum-running vehicles in his barn, as so many other farmers would do for a price. "Dad was an honest man, a man of ethics," Duquette said. "There was no price high enough to get him to sell out his moral principles."

Anatole Duquette was born on June 1, 1911, in Laprie, Quebec. He immigrated with his parents . . . when he was a young boy, and they settled just twenty miles south of the U.S.-Canadian border in Barton, Vermont, a farming community in Orleans County. They moved into a rambling old fourteen-room farmhouse and did their best to make a living, working long hours each day on their dairy farm. . . .

In a thick French-Canadian accent, Duquette reminisces about the old days, fondly recalling his youth and memories of his parents.

"There were few folks then who didn't have a batch of moonshine around the house," Duquette said warmly. "Some drank the brew to get drunk, others to relax, and some, like my father, as a ritual. Others called the moonshine 'medicine' and drank it when something ailed them. . . . Many folks made their own moonshine, and there wasn't just one way to make it. People had different recipes, and they brewed and distilled in all sorts of homemade contraptions." Some had elaborate stills that were capable of producing large amounts of moonshine. Others made it as his family did—in milk cans, the cans that farmers normally used to carry their milk to the creamery.

In the Duquette household, the concoction was mixed together in the kitchen and then the can was lugged upstairs to Anatole's bedroom, where it sat for about four days to soak. "My job was to shake it up every night to keep the mash from compacting on the bottom, which prevented it from

"'We used my bedroom because a stovepipe passed through it. We'd set the can next to the pipe to keep the mash warm and help it ferment into alcohol.'"

fermenting completely. The better the brew fermented, the stronger the final product," Duquette said. "We used my bedroom because a stovepipe passed through it. We'd set the can next to the pipe to keep the mash warm and help it ferment into alcohol. You had to keep that stuff hot," he pointed out, "and that wasn't an easy task during the winter months." Drafty Vermont farmhouses such as Duquette's had little, if any, insulation to help keep the winter cold out.

Once the mash had finished fermenting, the can was hauled back down to the kitchen. The contents were then poured through a strainer, which caught the mash solids while the liquid passed into a large kettle below. The kettle was put on the stove for distilling. Wasting nothing, the family fed the strainerful of mash to their poultry. . . .

"While many folks made moonshine, you didn't talk about it. People who bragged about their moonshining operations were typically all mouth, or weren't long for the business. Although most people around town minded their own business, there was always a handful of temperance-minded folk who were more than happy to volunteer whatever they heard about brewing or distilling to local, state, and federal lawmen.

"People making a few bottles or so for family use weren't a high priority for the lawmen. They were more interested in finding the renegade moonshiners who shunned the law and supplied the county with high-proof alcohol—stuff many times stronger than any beer that was crossing the border."

Desperate to avoid detection, these big-time still operators used a host of tricks to hide their work. Springtime sugaring operations were often just fronts for their distilling. Other moonshiners took to the deep woods with their homemade stills to avoid detection. . . .

While the Duquette moonshining operation was harmless, not everyone who moonshined was as peaceable as his family. People living in Barton were surprised when, on May 16, 1930, a decomposing body was found on the shores of Crystal Lake, a beautiful, clear lake just south of the village. *The Orleans County Monitor* reported the discovery:

"The body of a man later identified by the clothing as that of Grover Hemmings of Mount Airy, North Carolina, and Beebe, Quebec...."

Five days later, in the May 21 issue, the story behind the mysterious body's disappearance had been worked out by investigators:

"Mr. Hemmings has been employed in Beebe for some months as a stonecutter, but apparently was employed in smuggling on the side— for on the night of November 29, he and an unidentified companion were driving a liquor-laden car and given chase by officers from a point in Derby to a point out of Barton village, where the liquor car was ditched. In the dark, one man ran east toward Crystal Lake, only a few rods away, while the second party ran west to the woods above and across the railroad track. Officers followed some tracks both ways for a short distance, but saw there was no use following in the dark. A little later they thought they heard a cry for help from the lake and went to investigate, but seeing no signs of distress and hearing no further cries, believe the cry might be a ruse to get them from the car. The next day State's Attorney Miles and Sheriff Gray visited the spot upon the request of Custom officials, but inquiry of those living nearby and examination of the field, shore, and ice gave no clues to suspect the grim tragedy that apparently took place in the icy water of Crystal Lake the evening before."

The MATHEMATICS *of* PROHIBITION

DANIEL OKRENT

Prohibition is one of the most written-about periods in American history. Daniel Okrent, the first public editor of the New York Times *and a finalist for the 2004 Pulitzer Prize in history for his book* Great Fortune, *probed every aspect of the Great Experiment in his* Last Call: The Rise and Fall of Prohibition *(Scribner, 2010), not the least important of which was the very financial core of it at a time the nation was in the throes of financial chaos.*

The four-year march from the stock market crash to Repeal would turn out to be steady and irresistible, but that wasn't what most "wets" expected. As late as January 1932 many wet leaders and sympathetic journalists were still unconvinced that it was possible to secure a Twenty-First Amendment to unravel the Eighteenth. For one thing, in more than 140 years of constitutional history, not a single amendment had ever been repealed. Beyond that, as Charles Merz of the *New York Times*'s editorial board wrote, the imposing math faced by advocates provided "a devastating argument against the possibility of repeal."

On top of the two-thirds vote needed in each house of Congress (which could be stopped by just 33 dry senators), the requisite concurrence of three-quarters of the states was beyond daunting.

Ratification would require the positive action of both houses in each of 36 state legislatures. Thirteen of those 72 separate entities "could block repeal forever," Merz wrote in March 1931. "These 13 bodies, rightly apportioned, could exist in states containing approximately 5 percent of the country's population."

> *"Darrow and Beck both believed that the 'ghastly farce' could be ended only through revocation of the Volstead Act."*

That same winter, the eloquent James Montgomery Beck, who had come to refer to Prohibition as "this ghostly farce," asserted that "the Eighteenth Amendment cannot be repealed within a decade and possibly not within a generation."

Clarence Darrow pointed out in November 1931 that 34 U.S. senators represented states that were "hopelessly dry," and another 20 came from the "likely" dry, including such unpromising states as Alabama, Texas, Indiana and Georgia."

Darrow and Beck both believed that the "ghastly farce" could be ended only through revocation of the Volstead Act. That would require simple majorities in Congress and a presidential signature, which were daunting prospects in themselves. The possibility of achieving the much higher thresholds required by a Repeal amendment was a delusion.

This grim reality, said Darrow, "should convince the most stupid and optimistic Wet that if he can never buy a drink without repealing the Eighteenth Amendment, he had better start right in learning to make his own." Someone who saw Repeal as the only solution is "not against Prohibition," he concluded. "He's in favor of liquor, but against getting it."

In October 1929, Irving Fisher, the Yale economist who had remained Prohibition's leading intellectual defender, offered a comment that would earn him a place in American memory far more enduring than would his groundbreaking work on interest rates or even his loopy statistical analyses of beer's effect on the ability to memorize poetry.

"Stock prices have reached what looks like a permanently high plateau," said Fisher on October 15, nine days before the earth gave way on Black Monday. At least he truly believed it; his considerable fortune, invested in the market, followed the Dow Jones Industrial Average into a death spiral.

"'Stock prices have reached what looks like a permanently high plateau ...'"

This was a grave setback for the credibility of the dry movement's favorite scholar, but the effect of the Crash and the Depression on dry goals extended beyond personal humiliation. As businesses came apart, as banks folded, as massive unemployment and homelessness scoured the cities and much of the countryside, any remaining ability to enforce Prohibition evaporated.

President Herbert Hoover, trying to balance the budget while a hurricane rattled the scales, slashed funding for the already overburdened federal court system. The Prohibition Bureau cut agents' per diem from $6 to $5, and live training sessions were replaced with correspondence courses. The new Prohibition commissioner, a chemist named James M. Doran, had begun his tenure insisting he needed $300 million to enforce the law. But, with no more than $12 million made available to him, Doran defaulted to the reflexive optimism pioneered by his predecessor, Roy Haynes. Here's the good news, said Doran: In Prohibition's first nine years, the government had spent some $141 million on all forms of enforcement while collecting more than $460 million in fines, penalties and taxes—a profit, he boasted, of precisely $319,323,307.76.

A government running on fumes could have made good use of a humming, for-profit business in the side. It had not taken long for the Depression to corrode the inflow of federal tax collections. Revenue based on 1930 incomes was down 15%; the following year saw a 37% drop, and the year after that another 26%—compounded, it was a vertiginous 60% plunge in just three years.

In late 1928, E.B. White wrote an essay that touched on the amount New York City was spending "to enforce prohibition, which does not exist." A few months later, the *New York Telegram* posed the question "Where on Manhattan Island can you buy liquor?" The paper's answer: "In open saloons, restaurants, night clubs, bars behind a peephole, dancing academies, drugstores, delicatessens, cigar stores, confectioneries . . . ." It went on with 32 other suggestions, including paint stores, malt shops and moving van companies. "Times certainly are different," a housewife in lower Manhattan told an interviewer. "In the old days you never would have thought of buying your wine at the fish store."

[In 1930] the editor of the *Hutchinson News* in Kansas, a longtime dry, acknowledged the 10th anniversary of Prohibition by admitting that "there is 10 times as much drinking in Kansas today as there was 10 years ago . . . and consumption is increasing rather than diminishing."

In places where anything but neutral grain alcohol was hard to come by, grocery stores offered a flavoring substance called Peeko, available for 75 cents in rye, gin, rum, cognac, créme de menthe, and several other varieties. Just add these "perfect, true flavors" to your grain alcohol, the advertisements said, and drink up. On a far greater scale, the moonshine industry made some legitimate businesses vastly successful. Production of corn sugar, as essential to moonshine as grapes were to wine, soared from 152 million pounds in 1921 to 960 million pounds eight years later. In one four-year period, Standard Brands Inc. sold 64,000 packets of Fleischmann's Yeast in Richmond, VA, population 189,000. In Franklin County, Virginia, in the foothills of the Blue Ridge, where the population was only 24,000 (and, the Wickersham Commission reported, 99 out of 100 residents were involved in the moonshine business), Fleischmann's Yeast moved 2.5 *million* packages in the same four years.

It was not just a southern phenomenon. A single wholesale grocer in Rockford, IL, took delivery of two to three railroad carloads of corn sugar every week. Prohibition officials announced that they had seized 35,200 illegal stills and distilleries in 1929, plus 26 million gallons of mash, but judging from the amount of liquor washing over the country by that point, it was as if they had plucked a few blades of grass from a golf course.

The holes in the dike grew larger, and more numerous as well. Each time the president, the Prohibition Bureau, or any other agency announced a new effort, brought in new resources, or negotiated a new understanding with other governments, the flood of illegal alcohol found a new—and often more efficient—conduit.

Back in 1920, with Prohibition firmly situated in the Constitution and the Volstead Act already embedded in the law, the Anti-Saloon League spent $2.5 million in support of its cause. In 1933, as both that cause and the ASL faced a desperate emergency, it brought in a total of $122,000 to fund its activities, a brutal 95% decline. The most powerful pressure group the nation had ever known had been reduced to looking for nickels under the couch cushions.

The Twenty-First Amendment to the Constitution, which came up for debate in Congress in February 1933, was even more concise than the Eighteenth. The key words were the 15 that opened it: "The eighteenth article of amendment to the Constitution of the United States is hereby repealed." The remaining two clauses outlawed the transportation of intoxicating liquors into states that chose to forbid it and stipulated a ratification process requiring approval not by state legislatures but by state conventions called for this specific purpose.

"Prohibition officials announced that they had seized 35,200 illegal stills and distilleries in 1929, plus 26 million gallons of mash ..."

The first state convention to ratify the Twenty-First Amendment acted on April 10, in Michigan. By midsummer, 14 more states had ratified. On December 5, at 3:31 p.m. local time, Utah became the 36th state to ratify the Repeal amendment. At the age of 13 years, 10 months and 19 days, national Prohibition was dead. The official bootlegger in the Maryland State House was formally dismissed the same day.

On the GLOBAL WHISKEY TRAIL

no. 5

Distillation knows no boundaries. And, the taste for whiskey crosses virtually all borders worldwide. That means getting rid of the mindset that confines one's idea of whiskey primarily to the British Isles and North America.

In this set of essays, we look into the whiskey business in such disparate places as India, Japan, and South Africa.

ALL THE RAGE
in the RAJ

THOMAS BRUCE-GARDYNE

*The nation consuming the largest amount of whisky is
(a) England, (b) the United States, (c) Japan, (d) India?
Hint: It's D. The taste for the brown liquid gold that was
born during the Raj, the period of British colonial rule that
ran from 1858 to 1947, has continued to grow over the
generations since independence. Today, the world's second
most populous nation not only is a huge consumer of
imported spirits but has its own thriving industry. However,
not all is sweetness and light in India's relationship with
producer nations, as correspondent Tom Bruce-Gardyne
wrote in this essay, a version of which originally was
published in* Whisky Magazine *(issue 2, in 2003,
Norfolk, England).*

In consumption of spirits, Europe is as nothing compared to
India, the greatest whisky-drinking nation on earth. That
is, if you accept the Indian definition of the word "whisky,"
something the European Union refuses to recognize.

As a drink it does at least share the same color and strength as
Scotch, even if the taste can be varied in the extreme. Indian whisky
comes in a riot of styles, from the roughest rocket fuel imaginable to
a number of well-respected brands. None of them offer carbon-copy
Scotch, but one or two come pretty close, and as a general truism, the

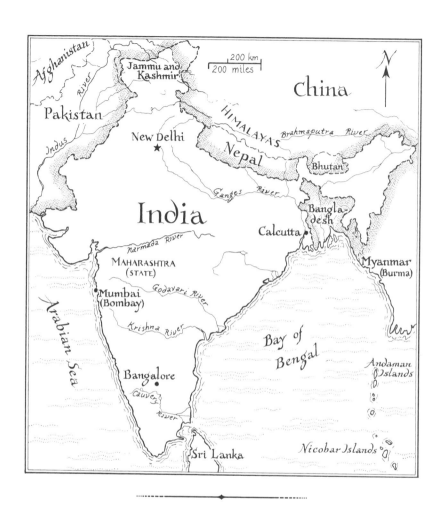

higher up the price ladder you climb, the closer to the real McCoy you'll get.

The fundamental difference is in the use of molasses rather than grain, which was banned by the old regime that ruled India in the years just after independence.

The regime, known as the license-permit Raj, decreed that grain was needed to feed the poor and could not be used to make spirits. The ban was lifted in 1995, and since then there have been indigenous grain whiskies made and even single malts.

The vast majority of Indian whisky still is molasses-based, however. As to how this affects quality, it all depends on the distiller. If the stills are worked too hard, the flavor of molasses tends to carry through into the spirit, giving it a raw, unbalanced feel, literally buzzing with congeners.

Like germs, these flavor-inducing compounds are good in small doses, but downright toxic in higher concentrations. Whether poorly made Indian whisky will kill you any quicker than other spirits is anyone's guess, but it can certainly give you a hangover you'll never forget.

Indian distilleries appear to have improved since the 1960s, when, according to the veteran BBC correspondent Mark Tully, "The Indian whisky most commonly served in Delhi was Black Night and was inevitably followed by a very black morning."

However, if cleanly distilled, you achieve a more neutral spirit than the barley bere of Scotland. So, to give the whisky some character, Indian distillers use a wide variety of flavorings.

With Scotch whisky, up to two-thirds of the character is said to derive from maturation. In India, only the most prestigious brands are given the benefit of a decent slumber in modern, air-conditioned warehouses. Trying to recreate the cold, dank conditions of Scotland in a country as hot and humid as India is costly, but essential to avoid ending up with rows of half-empty casks and a warehouse full of paralytic angels. One compromise solution is to blend in a proportion of Scotch which will have had the statutory three years maturation in Scotland.

While the ingredients and climate may be worlds apart, the image of Indian whisky is as Scottish as can be, with labels portraying chieftains, castles, and misty lochs. It somehow puts you in mind of "Brigadoon," Hollywood's appalling pastiche of the Highlands filmed in the 1950s. When the producer Arthur Freed went in search of a location, he famously concluded it would have to be shot in a studio for there was nowhere sufficiently Scottish in Scotland.

"In India, only the most prestigious brands are given the benefit of a decent slumber in modern, air-conditioned warehouses."

It is almost the same scenario with Indian whisky, where most brands of Scotch have long discarded any tattered tartan imagery. Thus in the West you have Johnnie Walker, the number one Scotch—a true global phenomenon promoted by actors as spokesmen, while in India you have the ever-popular Bagpiper brand whisky, pursued by McDowell's and a host of other clans.

Given the number of Scots who helped run the country at the height of the British Empire, it would be tempting to date this love of Scotland from the time of the Raj.

Yet, the drinks that sustained this huge ex-pat community were more often gin and tonic, favored for its anti-malarial properties, and brandy and soda. The real pioneers of Indian whisky were the local distillers themselves who naturally wanted to position their whiskies within range of the great flagship brands of Scotch in the hope that some of the allure might rub off.

As more Indians were able to afford international travel, they could see the gleaming rows of Chivas Regal and Johnnie Walker Black in the duty-free shops.

The number of whisky-drinkers in India who aspire to Scotch is many times the number who can afford to drink it. The cost of a bottle of The Famous Grouse in Bombay, for example, is equal to the city's minimum monthly wage. A more affordable option is to drink Teacher's or Vat 69 which are shipped out of Scotland in bulk to be diluted and bottled in India and cost roughly half the price. Even so, some 90 per cent of whisky drunk in India sells for less than $4.50 a bottle.

Compared to the local brew, Scotch whisky is massively discriminated against. Every bottle is hit with an import tariff of 340% the moment it arrives, after which an incredible cascade of taxes rains down on the journey from the port to the liquor store. It is said that for every dollar earned by an importer, nine more are made by the army of tax collectors.

As a result, the amount of bootlegged Scotch in India is colossal. This seeps in through diplomatic missions, cabin crews on airlines, and at all points along the country's 4,000-mile coastline.

However, for the many who get their hands on a cut-price case of Scotch, there is no guarantee it will be the real thing. According to a survey conducted in the mid-1990s, two out of three bottles of bootlegged Scotch were either adulterated or only Scottish by aspiration.

The classic example was Johnnie Walker Black, of which more is drunk in India in a year than is produced in the whole of Scotland; or so it was said.

And yet despite all that, India remains a tantalizing prospect for the Scotch whisky industry, and not just because the population is now officially over a billion.

It would be naive to dream of every Indian enjoying one dram of genuine Scotch a year; for most people it will remain beyond reach. But, the middle classes are growing, and the barriers to Scotch are slowly coming down.

Above all, the country's taste buds are already halfway there. The flavor of local whisky and the icons used to sell it make Scotch the obvious contender among imported spirits. Most people seem to know the difference between the two, and see Scotch as the drink to aspire to.

A WEE BIT *of* SCOTLAND *in* JAPAN

RICHARD HENDY

The average Westerner arguably thinks only of Europe and North America when it comes to whiskey. But, Asia is a huge consumer—and a growing maker—of whiskies of all sorts. India, for example, developed a raging thirst for single malts and other whiskies during the Raj, the period of British colonial rule that ended in 1947. It today is a hotbed of knockoffs of Scotch whiskies. However, Japan's modern-day distilling industry began just before World War II, heavily patterned after the traditional Scottish style; manufacturing sites were even selected to mimic the climate of the Highlands. In recent years, it has become a major player on the Asian scene and has been slowly getting acceptance in the global market. In this account, the writer and photographer Richard Hendy, an avowed Japanophile who lives in Tokyo and writes the blog **Spike Japan***, traces the history of the modern Japanese distilling movement.*

The very idea of Japanese whisky invites scoffery among some. Why, you might as well be drinking Belarusian cognac or Ukrainian port. And, it is true there is something unfashionably dogged about the Japanese determination to recreate Western wines and spirits on Eastern shores and mountains.

More than dogged, even; something quixotic, perhaps, almost

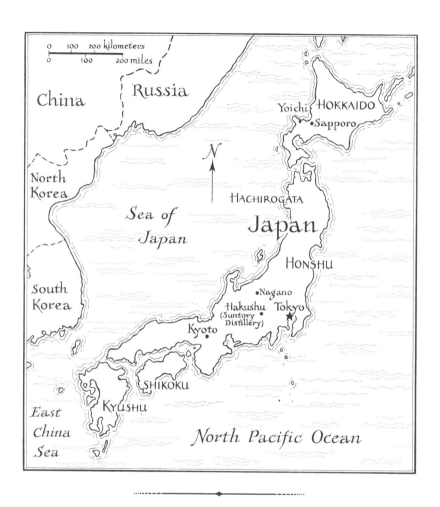

desperate, driven by subterranean urges of perceived inferiority and yet with something game, ambitious, and healthily iconoclastic thrown in.

My long quiescent interest in Japanese whisky was piqued by stumbling across an article that revealed that the 2008 World Whisky Awards' two most prestigious prizes had both gone to Japan. Suntory's Hibiki 30 won the best blended whisky award and Nikka's Yoichi 1987 20-year old malt the best single malt whisky award.

"If New World wines can cut it at the highest level and change the world's drinking habits, . . . why not Japanese whisky?"

Why should this not be a "Judgment of Paris" moment, a third of a century later, for the world of whisky? If New World wines can cut it at the highest level and change the world's drinking habits, . . . why not Japanese whisky?

There are any number of mostly miserable answers to that question. Foremost among them, to my mind, is that Japan will never in the foreseeable future be the sort of lifestyle superpower that in the broadest sense would give the backing to the brand. In the consumption troposphere that premium alcohol inhabits—below the stratosphere of watches and cars, antiques and art, which in turn lies below the mesosphere of noctilucent land—there has to be an easily conjured image, cliché if you like, that validates the purchase. With Old World wines and spirits, it might be the leisure of an arbor-shrouded long weekend lunch in the shadow of a handsome villa; with rum it might be the thud of calypso and reggae off the eaves of a thatched bar on the beach of a Caribbean hideaway; with Australian lager it might be the laid-back mateship of the Outback updated to a suburban garden barbecue setting; and, with Japanese beer, it could just about be the steely but chic-cut urban gray of a can of Asahi coupled with the brazen pertness and smug superiority of the assault on the Western dietary order that sushi represents.

But, you can't really make whisky urban, and the urban, the hyper-urban, and a good dose of urbanity is what post-war Japan has had to offer the world—or at least, what the world has been interested in taking, when it has been interested at all.

The intricacies of global branding would have been in the minds of precisely no one in 1894, however, when Nikka Whisky's founder, Masataka Taketsuru, was born, the third son of a sake brewer, in Hiroshima Prefecture. The two elder brothers went their own ways, and it was left to Masataka to study brewing at what is now Osaka University, where he developed an interest in Western alcohol.

Joining a brewer of Western spirits after graduation, the company president suggested he go and study the way of Scotch, which is how he ended up in the summer of 1919 in the applied chemistry department at Glasgow University, abetted in his quest for whisky perfection, so the Nikka mythologizing goes, by a nose broken at the age of seven and made supernaturally receptive to aromas, and then in the tiny Speyside village of Rothes. That is where or whereabouts he met the daughter of a Kirkintilloch doctor, Jessie Roberta ("Rita") Cowan, who he married in 1920, against the wishes of both sets of parents, in a registry office ceremony attended only by Rita's younger sister and two of her childhood friends.

He returned to Japan with Rita in tow in 1921 and spent much of the following decade at a brewer called Kotobukiya, which finally

shipped its first real whisky in 1929.

In 1934, free at last from a decade-long contact with Kotobukiya, Masataka and Rita departed for Yoichi, selected for its perceived similarity to Scotland in the harshness of its climate, the clarity of its waters, the abundance of peat, and its mist-shrouded mornings.

The distillery was completed the same year but the whisky needed years to mature and Masataka turned his hand to apple juice before the first whisky left the barrel in 1940. Yoichi still is a working distillery, but it also has turned itself into a well-executed tourist attraction. The museum, on which a lot of money has been lavished, was seductively lit, informative and engaging, and midway around the exhibits, should the visitor need refreshment, there's a very civilized bar with a vast selection of whiskies from around the world.

The museum makes great play of the romance between Masataka and Rita, referring to her more than once as Masataka's *shogai no hanryo*—lifelong companion—although he was to outlive her by almost two decades.

The foregrounding of Rita in a way serves as the ultimate imprimatur of Scottish authenticity on the whisky that Masataka created, and it's not hard to be touched by a twinge of sadness at her tale.

After arriving in Yoichi in 1934, she was never to return to Scotland and was kept under very watchful supervision by the *kempeitai* military police in World War II, which the museum, to its credit, does not gloss over. Nearly 50 by the time the war was over, Rita and Masataka never had children, although they did in very Japanese fashion adopt a nephew of Masataka, Takeshi. She died relatively young, aged 64, in 1961, just as Japan's high-growth era, which Nikka was by now in a perfect position to ride, was getting into full swing.

In his later years, it seems, Masataka became a typical mid-century Hemingwayesque plutocratic man of action, shooting bears from helicopters for sport and dying aged 85 in 1979, at the very apex of Japan's post-war love affair with whisky.

"Yoichi . . . 'hilarious, like a wee bit of Scotland on the other side of the world.'"

In 1989, Nikka bought the Ben Nevis distillery in Fort William, Scotland, in what looks suspiciously like a Bubble-inspired purchase of trophy real estate by Japanese interests along the lines of Pebble Beach in California and the Rockefeller Center in New York. An article in *The Scotsman* newspaper has a Ben Nevis representative describing Yoichi as "hilarious, like a wee bit of Scotland on the other side of the world."

Certainly the red-roofed malt drying kilns, stills, and warehouses in the distillery complex have an authentically dour Presbyterian heft to them. Nothing outside the distillery in the rest of Yoichi struck me as either particularly hilarious or as being like a wee bit of Scotland, however. The front gate of the distillery stands opposite an abandoned pachinko parlor.

Nikka, with around a fifth of the whisky market, has historically played second fiddle to the mighty Suntory, which has around two-thirds, and it was Suntory that devised a hierarchy of brands and attendant marketing strategies for them that were perfectly attuned to the hierarchy of the corporation and the ranks of the salarymen who were the prime consumers.

New company recruits started out drinking Suntory Red in the "Tory's Bar" whisky bars that sprung up in the big cities in the 1960s and 1970s (bafflingly pronounced *trisbaa*) and as they were promoted, convention allowed them to move on to pricier brands such as Kakubin ("square bottle") and, above all, Old, which led to the oft-repeated—and no doubt lost in translation—salaryman joke, "One day you'll be Old."

Whisky consumption in Japan peaked around 1980, at around 350,000 kiloliters, which works out very approximately to an impressive three liters for every man, woman and child in Japan. Tastes change, however, and whisky was already fast falling out of favor in the 1980s, before the collapse of the Bubble squeezed entertainment budgets and gave added impetus to the decline. Consumption has plummeted to around 100,000 kiloliters in recent years and there seems to be no easy way to arrest the decline.

Suntory's strategy seems to be to sell twentysomethings and thirtysomethings on single malts, with their whisky-as-wine tales of terroir and water and weather, and to woo young women with chocolate and single malt seminars ahead of Valentine's Day, and the brewer claims success in boosting sales of its Yamazaki single malt.

Which is all very well, but where does it leave the mass market for blended whiskies? And can the featherbedded elites of Tokyo and other metropolises really serve as a bridgehead to reach the less cocooned youth of the rest of the country, where the 4,000 yen cost of a bottle of Yamazaki 10-year old could easily represent half a day's pay?

In a country where lager made from corn, pea protein, soy protein, or soy peptides, rather than malt, has recently been all the rage because tax anomalies cause it to currently cost around $2.02 a 350ml can in a local convenience store, vs. $2.28 for a low-malt lager and $2.91 for the real full-malt thing, it seems unlikely.

The
SPIRITS *of* SOUTH AFRICA

MIKE DeSIMONE AND JEFF JENSSEN

South Africa has a solid reputation as a wine producing country, but its role in the global spirits community should not be overlooked. Mike DeSimone and Jeff Jenssen, also known as the World Wine Guys, are wine, spirits, food, and travel writers who have been published by such periodicals as Wine Spectator, The European, Saveur, *and* International Living. *While in search of fine wines in South Africa, they were pleasantly surprised by a spirit they came across, which prompted them to delve into the country's whisky niche for this book.*

J ust as there is much to be said for drinking wine in the land where the grape is grown, the whisky connoisseur often finds himself longing to enjoy a dram in the land where the grain is grown.

On misty autumn evenings, the smell of wet earth and burning leaves fills the air, and we find ourselves wishing for a return visit to, well, not somewhere obvious like Edinburgh or Glasgow, but . . . Cape Town. A rich melting pot of culture and cuisine, South Africa is well known for her world class wines, but few people know that much of

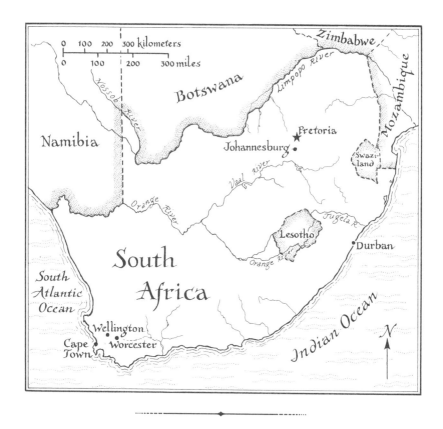

the grain blended into Scottish whisky in the not so distant past was shipped from the maize and wheat fields of Wellington, a short drive north of the Cape.

As we were waiting for some friends at a wood-paneled, vaguely nautical-themed bar in Cape Town's Victoria and Albert Waterfront and trying to decide what to drink, a fellow patron suggested we sample a local whisky, Three Ships. Although we expected it to taste like mouthwash, we ordered it anyway. We were instantly rewarded with a textured heavyweight crystal glass filled halfway with a deep amber jewel bearing a nose of fruit and peat, a silky-smooth flavor of lightly-toasted toffee, and a long, elegant finish.

We were delighted to learn that the Three Ships 5 Year Old is a combination of South African whisky *and* Scotch whisky, which seemed perfect to us that in this melting pot of a city poised between two oceans even the whisky has a dual pedigree.

Three Ships is brewed at the James Sedgwick Distillery in Wellington. It is named for Captain James Sedgwick, a mariner who arrived in Cape Town in 1850 and founded J. Sedgwick and Company, a purveyor of liquor, tobacco, and cigars.

Cape Town, a key point on the Spice Route—and, in fact, all sea travel between Europe and the East—and its environs are a fascinating blend of English, Dutch, French, Indian, Indonesian, and, of course, local indigenous African culture. The distillery itself is a sight to behold, with its high stone walls and enigmatic pagoda. Antique copper Coffey stills remain in use, and the whisky ages in a combination of new American oak and used bourbon and sherry barrels in an arcana of blending tradition.

The distillery sits close to Bain's Kloof Pass, which runs between Wellington and Ceres, the latter named for the Roman goddess of grain. It offers views of extensive seas of wheat and barley as well as the Atlantic and Indian Oceans. Gazing, with a glass of whisky in hand, at the distant bodies of water coming together at the Cape of Good Hope, one cannot help but think back to Captain Sedgwick and his undertakings even though little is known about him.

Family records indicate that a brother, Thomas, made his way to Bombay and died young after first having promoted mulberry trees for the silk trade. Another brother, William, was a doctor who initially worked in London with the noted surgeon Josef Lister, the founder of antiseptic surgery and for whom Listerine is named. A fourth sibling, Charles, settled in Boston and became a prominent journalist. James himself, settling in Cape Town, between the worlds inhabited by his family members. He imported, exported, and produced wines and spirits in addition to authoring two books about sailing.

Captain Sedgwick originally produced brandy, a spirit distilled from wine. At some point he began making whisky, in 1886 purchasing the distillery in Wellington in the heart of the grain belt.

There was obviously a demand for domestic spirits in that era. The Hungarian-born businessman Alois Hugo Nellmapius had opened the Hatherley Distillery on his farm in 1883, producing gin and whisky under the Volkshoop label. After Nellmapius' death, a competitor named Sammy Marks took over the distillery and other operations. A photo of Nellmapius still hangs in Marks's 1884 mansion-cum-museum outside Pretoria in the only wholly preserved Victorian house in the country. House tours end with tea and scones, although a dram of domestic whisky might be more appropriate.

At that time, Dutch immigrant Jan van Ryn's eponymous Cape Town brandy-making operation, which still is operational in nearby Stellenbosch, was nearly forty years old. The Suez Canal, connecting the Mediterranean and Red seas and cutting South Africa and the Cape of Good Hope off of the Europe-to-Asia sailing itinerary—

had opened in November 1869, just two years after Erasmus Jacobs discovered the first of many diamonds on the banks of the Orange River. If diamonds and then gold and other precious metals had not been turned up from the earth near Cape Town, it is likely the once-thriving metropolis would have gone the way of many other port cities with the introduction of air travel, or American downtowns with the advent of the shopping mall.

"Races were held every year to see which ship could bring back to London the first of the new tea harvest in China."

Before the arrival of steamships, which could easily ply the canal, trade between Europe and Asia relied on great sailing ships known as clippers. Races were held every year to see which ship could bring back to London the first of the new tea harvest in China. All these clippers stopped in Cape Town.

One of the greatest of them was *Cutty Sark,* built in 1869, the same year the Suez Canal was completed. One of only three original clippers which still exist, *Cutty Sark* (Scottish slang for a type of short shirt) figures strongly in the lore of Scotch whisky. Cutty Sark Original Scots Whisky, in its memorable green bottle bearing an image of the clipper on its yellow label, was many a man's whisky of choice before the current boom of premium and super premium liquors took hold of the marketplace. Throughout the years, it has made many appearances in film, television, and music, and it is remembered with nostalgia by gentlemen of a certain age. The brand, introduced in 1923, seems to have fallen out of favor among younger whisky lovers, and its image may remain moored alongside its namesake clipper, a quaint tourist attraction for those who have a taste for the past. Or not. The original ship is undergoing a renovation, so perhaps the entry of high-end 12-, 15-, 18-, and 25-year-old blends will bring Cutty Sark the whisky back into the spirits race.

But we digress, an easy thing to do when sipping South Africa's first single grain whisky, an oaky Bain's Cape Mountain, bearing warm notes of caramel and spice, and pondering the nation's distillation history.

To quote Andy Watts, master distiller at Sedgwick where Bain's is produced, speaking of its inspiration: "At its base the road cuts into the mountain slopes and winds its way through pine forests and *fynbos* where many protea species grow on the higher mountain slopes. The whisky pays tribute not only to one of the most picturesque and magnificent passes in South Africa but also honors Andrew Geddes Bain, the creative mind behind its construction." The pass was completed in 1853, and this feat of engineering is now a national monument.

Multiple factors in the mid- to late-19th Century led to a burgeoning population in South Africa, mostly males and many in need of drink. Brandy was extremely popular at this time, and the phylloxera epidemic of 1859 devastated the French wine industry and, in turn, the French brandy industry, which helps to explain the preponderance of South African distilleries at that time. Unfortunately, the dreaded vine-destroying aphids made their way to the Cape Winelands about 25 years later, causing serious damage to many a wine farm's crops. As grape growth and winemaking took a nosedive, so did the ability to make brandy. And, if one already has a distillery in the center of the country's breadbasket, why not switch over production to whisky? Especially when there are an enormous number of miners and soldiers on hand, two groups who throughout history are known to have enjoyed their fermented and distilled beverages.

Shortly after the discovery of diamonds and gold in South Africa, Cecil Rhodes and his brother Herbert arrived on the scene. They originally worked on a cotton farm in Natal, north of the Cape, but when diamond fever swept the region, the brothers headed for the diamond fields of what then was known as the Transvaal. Cecil, one of nine children of an English vicar, had been shipped off to South Africa to earn a living because he had been too sickly as a youngster to attend school. He went on to head the DeBeers diamond monopoly in 1888, received a Royal Charter for his British South Africa Trading Company in 1889, held the position of prime minister of the Cape Colony from 1890 through 1896, was one of the founding fathers of both South Africa and Rhodesia, and funded the renowned Rhodes Scholarship. Countless books have been written about his accomplishments, but the two which interest us the most discuss his widely disputed drinking habits.

According to Rhodes' companion and secretary, Gordon LeSeur, Rhodes liked his drink. In his 1914 tome, *Cecil Rhodes: The Man and His Work* (McBride, Nast and Co., 1914), LeSeur informs the reader that his employer drank a quart of mixed champagne and stout every morning. Obviously a good start to the day, because in addition to that, "He liked his champagne in a tumbler and would absentmindedly drink glass after glass. He also drank five or six liqueur glasses of Kümmel after his meals."

If this is what the nation's founder imbibed on a daily basis, one can only imagine the tippling habits of the common man. Of course, there are two sides to every story, and Philip Jourdan's *Cecil Rhodes: His Private Life,* originally published in 1923 and reprinted by BiblioLife in 2009, paints a picture of abstemiousness, at least from the heavy drinker's point of view. Defending his friend and confidant against previously published claims of overindulgence, Jourdan writes, "His first drink of the day was at lunch; then he had generally a glass of whiskey and soda . . . ." Clearly a man after Carry Nation's own heart, reserving his drinking for later in the day and cutting it with soda at that!

Whatever the case, of the two Rhodes brothers who made their way to South Africa, Cecil clearly is the one who had a healthier relationship with alcohol. Of Herbert, LeSeur tells us of his tragic death in 1879, after a move to Central Africa: "He was pouring a drink from a demijohn of gin, when a spark from his pipe ignited the spirit, causing the demijohn to explode and set his clothing alight." Despite throwing himself in a nearby river to douse the flames, he did not survive the extensive burns.

Gin drunk from a demijohn clearly was domestic gin, no doubt from Alois Nellmapius' Hatherley Distillery, but Cecil's whisky could have come via ship from Scotland. It also is known that he smoked only cigarettes from Cairo, and, since true Champagne comes only from one place, it is most likely Rhodes drank imported spirits as well. If he were alive today and not drinking his whisky straight up, it is probable he would enjoy Harrier, a three-year-old malt whisky which is another South African and Scottish blend. It is one of the most popular domestic brands, with a reputation as the one to use when mixing.

In addition to the mining situation, or more to the point because of it, there was a war going on in South Africa in the 1880s, the First Boer War. Unhappy with colonization by the British, the Boers—farmers who were descendants of Dutch settlers—began moving inland in a migration known as "The Great Trek." Once precious stones and minerals were discovered, the British laid claim to much of the land the Boers had made their own. War broke out, and reinforcements from back home flooded the Cape. There also were continual battles with the indigenous Zulu nation. With the influx of legitimate soldiers, mercenaries, and miners came those industries which cater to the needs of traveling men: saloons and brothels. Think San Francisco in 1849, but multiply exponentially. Now subtract legitimate news sources and photography expanding the tales of the lawlessness of this place at the bottom of the map. Then add the Suez Canal, negating the need to drop anchor in this place unless you really wanted or needed to. This was truly the time to be in the business of making brandy, whisky, and gin on the home front.

Thanks to the pioneering efforts of the likes of Cecil Rhodes and Paul Kruger, leader of the Boer resistance to the British, and the man for whom Kruger National Park is named, and the forces of history, time, and outside influence, Cape Town and indeed all of South Africa are very different places than they were in those days.

The original stills and aging barrels at the Sedgwick Distillery in Wellington today are used within a state of the art facility, which received the Wellington Tourist Board Trophy for Most Attractive Industrial Site in 2000 and is open for distillation and visits.

In addition to blended South African and Scotch whiskies, the Sedgwick Distillery also is noted for the first whisky whose malt and grain are grown, distilled, and matured in South Africa, the aforementioned Bourbon Cask Finish. Three Ships Whiskies have won a multitude of awards over the years. Unfortunately, just as a prophet is never revered in his hometown, many of the people of South Africa are not aware of this gem at their doorstep. Although more than two million liters of whisky are consumed within South Africa each year, Scotch and Canadian brands lead the way.

To the true connoisseur, value is directly proportional to scarcity: The idea that the only complete fleet of Three Ships in the United

States may well rest within the glass-fronted confines of our circa-1885 wine and liquor closet makes an in-home tasting of Select, 5 Year Old and Bourbon Cask Finish a highly prized invite, even in hard-to-impress New York City. Winemakers, editors, and friends from the worlds of wine and cuisine stop by for dinner or drinks on a regular basis, and at the end of the meal—or before, while palates are still fresh—we delight in sharing a few drops of the otherwise unobtainable South African nectar with our esteemed guests.

Sorting through our scribbles and jottings and printouts while judiciously sipping a glass of luscious Three Ships Bourbon Cask Finish, barely wetting our lips with the precious remaining drops, we note the history of the Sedgwick family with great amusement: William's connection to Listerine, which Three Ships most definitely does not resemble, and Thomas's involvement with silk, which it definitely does. And let's not forget Charles, the prominent American journalist. Only through our common profession did we come into contact with this little known jewel of South Africa, and the history and legacy of his brother, Captain James.

"In addition to blended South African and Scotch whiskies, the Sedgwick Distillery also is noted for the first whisky whose malt and grain are grown, distilled, and matured in South Africa . . ."

As the liquid levels in our bottles falls lower and lower, and the tastes get smaller and smaller, we regale our guests with tales of our last trip to South Africa and simultaneously plan the next if for no other reason than to replace our precious stock.

HOW TO...

no. 6

There is more—much more, in fact—to the world of whiskies than merely sipping the products. In the following essays, experts in the field explain the ins and outs of collecting, tasting, and—all right, drinking.

...BECOME *a* COLLECTOR

JENNIFER HARPER

If you can restrain yourself enough not to drink away your stash of fine whiskies, you might become a collector of special expressions of the amber gold. There is, of course, a lengthy list of details that need attention. Jennifer Harper, writing in Scottish Field *magazine, explains how to join that special breed that prefers to keep their bottles unopened, gaining flavor and value.*

Every day, the world over, people raise a glass of whisky and toast to good health, success, or even just to seeing through another day. Whisky is a world-class drink that is given the same respect on all sides of the globe. But, not everyone is too happy to open a bottle. Some people prefer to buy a bottle, knowing the quality of the beverage inside, but will let both its flavor and its value improve over time.

This is the whisky collector, someone who generally has a fine appreciation and enjoyment for drinking whisky, but also has a finger on the pulse when it comes to recognizing a release that will prove to be an auction room favorite in years to come. McTear's auctioneers in Glasgow have become renowned for holding four key whisky, wine and port auctions annually, with collectors from all over the world making the journey to Scotland to bid.

"We find there are people from all different backgrounds buying whisky," says Andrew Bell, Head of Whisky and Wine with McTear's. "At our most recent sale we had one collector from the north of England who has over 1,000 bottles, and another serious collector who came over from Italy to make specific purchases. We find that collectors do their research and will know what they are going to bid for when they arrive."

Without a doubt, no whisky auction would be complete without the name Macallan in the listings. "Macallan has been one of the strongest whiskies," says Andrew. "We recently sold a 50-year-old Macallan for £4,400 [US$7,206]. Every now and again we get a 1946 or 1948 vintage which will usually go for around £1,200 [US$1,927]." He adds, "Now and again another whisky will claim the top spot. We sold an 1850 Mutter Bowmore for £29,000 [US$46,593] in our September 2007 sale and a 62-year-old Dalmore for over £25,000 [US$40,166] in 2002."

" 'At our most recent sale we had one collector from the north of England who has over 1,000 bottles …' "

These prices may be out of reach for the majority of collectors, but Andrew says that anyone trying to start a collection could begin with a £50 [$US80] budget.

"My advice would be to keep your first spend to below £50 and to look for a few smaller bottlings here and there," he says. "If your budget increases then look at splashing out on distillery-owned and limited editions. There is quite a whisky community out there, so you often hear of forthcoming releases through word of mouth.

I am secretary of the Glasgow Whisky Club, and when we meet up everyone will have some information to share about a whisky, so it's good to join a club like that or attend tastings. It is a good way to meet like-minded souls."

A look through [one month of] McTear's whisky sales results proves there are bargains to be found. An SS Politician Decanter sold for £85 [$137], while two bottles of Port Ellen 1978, both from the Decanter Collection, sold for £80 [US$128] and £90 [US$145].

By coincidence, each of these features decanters. But, how important is original presentation packaging?

"The original packaging is great to have, but it does not affect the price a great deal," confides Andrew. "I would never expect to see bottles from 50 years ago with perfect boxes and perfect labels. I would never give a bottle a lower estimate if the packaging was missing or damaged. It is what is on the inside that counts."

The question of the airtight quality of the decanter must also be considered.

"Like wine, whisky does start to fall away once the bottle has been opened, though it is much slower with whisky. This is why you should never save the last dram in your bottle for a special occasion. By the time you drink it, it might not be the beautiful malt you first opened."

As with any collection, Andrew suggests buying a whisky that you would like to drink yourself in case its value does not greatly increase and you decide to keep it. However, he adds that you must also store it correctly in order to preserve the contents.

"You should keep the bottle upright so that the cork does not touch the spirit and keep it at a constant temperature away from bright light or electricity. My own collection is hidden at the back of a wardrobe," he says with a smile.

... TASTE WITHOUT
"Cups of Despair"
JIM MURRAY

*Connoisseurs of spirits, wine, and beer rarely argue
over one point: The glasses used in tastings are a huge
component in the experience. Jim Murray, the renowned
English spirits writer, has come across tastings using all
sorts of vessels about which he has written for such books
as* The Art of Whisky, Complete Book of Whisky,
Classic Bourbon, Tennessee & Rye, *and his ongoing
work* The Whisky Bible. *He waxed philosophically, and
with some disdain, on the topic in this essay published
in the inaugural issue of* Whisky Magazine *(published
December 1, 1999, Norfolk, England).*

It has happened three times so far this year. It will doubtless
happen again. What we are talking about here is something so
horrific, so utterly contemptible and breathtakingly philistine,
that I'm not sure bringing the topic up is a good idea for the more
squeamish among you.

Plastic tasting glasses.

I know that those three words, in that particular order, are likely to
send you scampering to another page for sanctuary, but I'll take the chance.

If there has been any one more singularly dastardly device devised
in the history of mankind, I have yet to find it. There you are, at some

plush restaurant or hotel waiting to host a tasting. You have organized the whiskies, some of which are absolute classics or aged and rare. The first dinner-jacketed whiskyites are taking inquiring and hopeful steps towards the door, backing off when they realize they are not yet welcome, and then circling like hungry sharks for the next 10 minutes.

Then I discover why the aroma drawing them is so very strong. Most of the whisky is being tipped onto the tablecloth. The tulip-shaped glasses I had asked for, and been assured I would get, are nowhere to be seen. In their place are tiny cups that have descended from the same primitive evolutionary tree as thimbles.

The staff, embarrassed but doing their best, splutter apologies because they can't get the bottles into the cups. This begs the question of how the hell the guests are going to be getting their noses in there.

Finally, I collar the organizer, who had secretly hoped I wouldn't notice the runt-sized tumblers until it was too late.

"Er," he says, "couldn't get any of those nosing glasses, so I thought these would do."

Well, he thought wrong. Fortunately, each time it has happened so far there has been a bar or restaurant nearby, so emergency wine glasses

have been ferried in. Connoisseurs have thus been saved from a fate worse than death.

Nothing, for me, ruins a good whisky tasting more than poorly selected glasses. And plastic ones are the worst of all. First, they are too small actually to allow the aroma of whisky to develop, and the only smell that is detectable is unpleasantly synthetic. And, although the event may be a tasting, without first savoring—or sometimes, alas, recoiling from—the aroma, the experience is incomplete. It is, as I have always said, the foreplay before the most intimate of moments.

One organizer I admonished for offering such poisoned chalices sniffed at me, "Well, no one has complained before."

Probably because they were too speechless.

"Would you put wine in that?" I demanded.

"Well, as a matter of fact, no," was his faltering reply.

"Then why is it OK for whisky?"

He blinked and then nodded as the point sank in.

Of course, the juice of the grain is still regarded in many quarters as something inferior to that of the grape, though the perception is slowly—almost imperceptibly—changing. There have

"Nothing, for me, ruins a good whisky tasting more than poorly selected glasses. And plastic ones are the worst of all."

even been attempts to devise the "perfect" whisky glass. Riedel does one, though I avoid it with a vengeance: the stubby stem makes it impossible to get your hands underneath and warm the whisky in order to put it through its paces. When, unbeknown to me, a picture of this glass ended up on the cover of my German-edition book *Whisky & Whiskey* I nearly died.

So, if you're at a tasting and all you are offered are sad little medicine cups, give the organizers hell. And, if I happen to be conducting the event, then form a disorderly queue behind me.

...UNDERTAKE HOME VATTING

MORITZ KALLMEYER

Vatting whiskey is, simply put, the practice of mixing several different whiskies to achieve a new taste. The trick is you don't have to be a large commercial distiller or even a micro-distiller to get involved in the practice. And, you don't have to be a resident of the major whiskey-producing regions of the world. Take Moritz Kallmeyer, founder of South Africa's Drayman's Brewery and Distillery and a recognized expert on vatting. Here is his company's take on the practice.

Keeping oak barrels at home filled with an assortment of alcoholic beverages is an ancient custom. Keeping the cask at least half full and replenishing it with "fresh stock" is called a Solera process.

A traditional Solera system in a cellar would have a barrel stack ranging from the youngest at the top to the oldest at the bottom.

A proportion of whisky is removed from the barrels in the bottom row for bottling. These, in turn, are topped up from the row above and so on. The very top row is topped up with the youngest whisky.

In this way a very consistent product over many years can be produced. The bottom barrels will, thus, always contain a portion of the original whisky used in the Solera. Nowadays barrels are stored side-by-side, and the product is transferred with a pump.

Whisky, brandy, port, sherry, mead and also beer—especially lambic, stale old ale and Flanders red—lends itself well to this keeping method. But, for now I want to introduce you to Drayman's Solera Whisky.

For the last few years the living cask has been my new hobby at home and has now been transformed into a small whisky business. It is a perfectly legal hobby here to "make" your own whisky at home—so long as "make" is defined as the blending of whiskies which you have bought from a liquor store and then maturing it in your own cask or casks. Obviously you can't sell it either, unless you have an alcohol manufacturing license.

"Vatted malt" means a blend—or vatting—of only single malt whiskies from various distilleries. The advent of vatting demonstrates an understanding of maturation and shows how the first commercial blenders were trying to impose quality and consistency in their products.

Vatting was widely practiced in private homes. In 1864, Charles Tovey wrote of how, "in a gentleman's cellar" one would find a hogshead (must have had a lot of friends!) containing four or five malts (whisky) which would be replenished with "any whisky that

"It is a perfectly legal hobby here to 'make' your own whisky at home—so long as 'make' is defined as the blending of whiskies which you have bought from a liquor store and then maturing it in your own cask or casks."

is particularly approved (of)" when the volume dropped below half.

This Solera method of vatting was expanded upon by Professor George Saintsbury in his book *Notes on a Cellar* (1920). The Professor's cask contained Clynelish, The Glenlivet, Glen Grant, Talisker, and Islay. The idea has been revived by Richard Joynson at Loch Fyne, whose "Living Cask" has been evolving since 1988.

"Bearing in mind that maturation accounts for 70 percent of the flavor of any whisky, you now can re-create a complex whisky at home with vatting."

Vatted malts are more than just pure malt blends without adding grain whisky, as practiced by the puristic portion of its followers. Vatted malts are about combining different levels of complexity to create different flavor combinations.

For example, Glenfiddich Solera Reserve 15-year old is stored in huge Solera vats that, in common with those in Jerez, Spain, are always kept at least half-full. This method of fractional blending not only gives consistency between bottlings but builds in extra layers of flavor—far more complex than conventional finishing.

Most Speyside whiskies have gradually dropped their peating levels in the past few decades, and many are also noticeably lighter in style. The complex, almost oily character and the combination of floral notes, smoke and silky palate so valued by devotees of the old style, have largely disappeared. Bearing in mind that maturation accounts for 70 percent of the flavor of any whisky, you now can re-create a complex whisky at home with vatting.

If "Vatted malt" implies using only single malt whisky, then perhaps "Solera blend" would be an appropriate term to use where a mixture of both malt and grain whisky is used in a Solera cask. A "Solera blend" is a more affordable approach to the hobby and allows the blender the freedom to use malt-whisky, grain-whisky and blends thereof to create his own unique flavors.

AND, NOT TO BE FORGOTTEN...
no. 7

Not everything can be neatly placed into specific categories, but that does not diminish their importance to a field such as the manufacture and consumption of spirits.

With that in mind, here is a small collection of looks at some offbeat people, places, and processes.

The
INESTIMABLE
JERRY THOMAS

DAVID WONDRICH

Beyond those who make the whiskies of the world, there is another sort who makes all their efforts worthwhile: the bartender extraordinaire. Back in 1862, New York City's top bartender—Jerry Thomas, known as "The Professor"— wrote a book called How to Mix Drinks, or The Bon Vivant's Companion. *It became the bible of sophisticated bartenders for more than a half century, and Thomas became known as the Father of American Mixology. A modern-day disciple, David Wondrich, lavished praise on Thomas as he himself became a major player in the resurgence of cocktail society in America. Wondrich is a founding member of the Museum of the American Cocktail and much in demand as author and lecturer. This essay originally appeared in his* Imbibe: From Absinthe Cocktail to Whiskey Smash *(A Perigee Book, New York, 2007). It picks up in New York City in the raucous 1860s after Thomas had knocked around the globe for a while, acquiring experience and ideas for his own establishment that catered to the high society as well as the lesser celebrity drinkers of the day.*

His run at the top started off auspiciously enough when, after a couple years at the Metropolitan and a quick sporting jaunt to London (the Heenan-Sayers fight; according to what he told Alan Dale, this was only the first of many visits), the thirty-year-old Jerry Thomas opened his own place, just a couple of blocks up from the Metropolitan at 622 Broadway.

This elaborate establishment was in the same building as Laura Keene's New Theater and probably, as was customary, attached to it. Certainly La Keene (the most popular actress of her day; and the only one to run her own theater company) displayed no conspicuous Temperance proclivities that would have prevented the usual connection being made. In which case, Thomas might have noticed, one night in 1861, an intense, dreamy-eyed man on the edge of middle age pop in for a quick Gin Cocktail or Santa Cruz Sour.

Some old friends of Stephen Foster were in town from Pittsburgh and had managed to extricate the songwriter, then just beginning his final slide into destitution and death, from the East Side liquor groceries where he was killing himself on adulterate rum. After dinner at the St. Nicholas, they treated him to a play at Laura Keene's. I can't imagine Foster handling the second half without a bracer.

Foster wasn't the only celebrity to come within the Professor's orbit at 622. In October 1860, Queen Victoria's son Edward, the Prince of Wales, visited New York. The reception he received was overwhelming—for a free people, Americans of the day were shocking royalists. Poor Edward's hotel, the Fifth Avenue at Twenty-third and Fifth, was so besieged by crowds that he was essentially trapped there.

In 1902, however, an old newshound by the name of George Forrester Williams published an interesting story to the effect that one night during the prince's visit, he [Williams] and Mortimer

Thomson, a fellow scribe who had achieved a fair degree of fame for the dialect humor he wrote under the pseudonym "Doesticks," managed to achieve a private audience with his Royal Highness. Upon perceiving how miserable the man was to be trapped in his hotel, they suggested sneaking him out the back way for a quick tour of the neighborhood. He immediately assented. Since the crowd was watching the front—royalty doesn't use the back door—things went off without a hitch. The trip stalked briskly down Twenty-third Street toward Sixth Avenue, a street of saloons, gambling houses, minstrel theater, dance halls, and oyster houses. Real New York. As they turned up Sixth, Doesticks posed the question: "Have you ever drunk a mint julep, sir?"

> *"'Thomson led the prince into a famous barroom presided over by the no less famous Jerry Thomas, one of the greatest artists in his line or time.'"*

No, the prince had not. Yes, he would. And here's the kicker: "Thomson led the prince into a famous barroom presided over by the no less famous Jerry Thomas, one of the greatest artists in his line or time." High Royal Highness watched the "elaborate and picturesque style of manufacture practiced by the mixers of elixirs in those antebellum days with profound curiosity and admiration," took a sip, said, "Why, it's only a lemonade, after all," revised his opinion as the Julep-glow suffused him, and pronounced it "very, very nice." End of anecdote. Now, if there were two people who should have met, they were the Prince of Wales and Jerry Thomas; they had much in common, from a deep curiosity into the composition of drinks to an interest in the operation of the rules of probability to an unshakable personal dignity leavened with humor. But, the details, the details. What was Thomas doing up there on Sixth Avenue when his bar down near Broadway was open? And why is there no other record of this bar? And, most of all, what the hell was he doing putting lemon in his Julep? Other than that, the story is possible. But Williams might not have told the whole of it (and, for the record, there are plenty of lemon Juleps to be found in the literature).

> *". . . what the hell was he doing putting lemon in his Julep?"*

But according to one Richard Doolittle, a New York businessman, the outing was rather wilder than Williams, who has things ending quickly and sedately, let on. As Doolittle recalled in 1892, the prince and his party ended up downtown, rather worse for the wear, and—as happens in these situations—got separated. "The heir to Britain's throne wandered, unattended, into a . . . resort and produced to make things pretty lively," whereupon "the bartender started in to squelch him, and would have done so effectually had I not taken charge of the roisterer and piloted him back to his party."

Jerry Thomas's bar was downtown, it should be noted, and I doubt he was disposed to take any guff from splificated customers, heirs to the throne or not.

It was while he was at 622 Broadway that Thomas did something no American bartender had ever done before and put the unruly mass of formulae that every skilled mixologist carried around in his head down on paper.

Barkeepers tended to regard their recipes as trade secrets, not to be exposed to the *vulgus profanum*. For whatever reason, though, Jerry Thomas broke the old. The book certainly didn't hurt his star power, anyway, on the strength of which he was able to go to the Occidental [Hotel] in San Francisco in 1863. . . . Why he would want to leave a thriving bar of his own to do so is another question. Perhaps the Leland brothers, who ran both that hotel and the Metropolitan and hence knew his work well, simply made him an offer he couldn't refuse. But I suspect there was more to it: In the summer of 1863, as the Civil War was raging, the draft came to New York, and Jerry Thomas was highly eligible. The sporting milieu he was a part of looked unkindly on the war to begin with, and a bolt-hole in San Francisco must have seemed pretty attractive. Even more attractive, however, was the vast and vulgar spectacle that was unfolding 200 miles to the east in Virginia City, Nevada, where a city of 30,000 had sprung up overnight on top of the massive mountain of silver known as the Comstock Lode. By 1864, Thomas was there, either (as local legend has it) at the famous Delta Saloon or at the Spalding Saloon on C Street, where the City Directory found him—or, of course, at both. Wherever he wielded his shaker, he would've known local newspaperman Samuel Clemens, who was just then beginning his

"After two years our bar receipts ran $400 a day, and the way people used to drop in to look at Mr. Thomas Nast's pictures was a pleasing thing to us . . ."

literary career and didn't think a Whiskey Cocktail would bite, much. Unfortunately, the *Territorial Enterprise*, Mark Twain's paper, burned in one of Virginia City's frequent fires, and all its archives and most of its back issues with it.

In 1865, as soon as the shooting stopped, Jerry Thomas was back in New York, operating a saloon with his brother, George, at the very fashionable address of Fifth Avenue and Twenty-second Street, just south of Madison Square. The space, at 937 Broadway, was "a narrow strip about 15 feet wide and 150 feet deep," as *The New York Times* described it, that ran through the block and had a second entrance on Fifth. "It was a great place," the Professor recalled in 1882.

"After two years our bar receipts ran $400 a day, and the way people used to drop in to look at Mr. Thomas Nast's pictures was a pleasing thing to us, who stood ready to serve them with what they wished to drink when they were done. You remember the Hogarth prints, the full set, without mercy—the fine illustration on steel of Mr. and Mrs. Gyges that—what's his name?—the father of history— Herodotus—tells about, and the oysters and the rarebits, cooked special, to say nothing of the chops, and the fat and lean looking glasses (for the first time), and the tables that ran along all in a row, as cozy as chickens on a roost and not near so crowded."

Between the art and the drinks and the free lunch and the steaks and chops and the funhouse mirrors, for a few years there the Thomas brothers ran what was probably the most famous freestanding bar in America. According to an 1871 article in *Appleton's Magazine*, it was a "favorite resort of the American *jeunesse doreé*" and, after the bar at the nearby Fifth Avenue Hotel, "probably the most frequented place after dark" in the city.

Things were so good that for once the Professor stayed put. In fact, in 1867 he even got married. Henrietta Bergh Waites, a New York City native, was a widow some five years younger than her husband with a teenage daughter, also named Henrietta. Before long, she had another child to take care of: Milton, or Minturn—records differ—was born the next year. A daughter, Louise, followed some three years after that. For a time, anyway, Jerry Thomas was a family man and a successful businessman—a proper Victorian. He even took to joining things—he turned up as a member of the stuffy Wine & Spirit Traders' Society and the rather less tony Fat Men's Association (at a portly but still mobile 205 pounds, he was one of the lightest members).

> "*... Jerry Thomas's comic gallery is as well visited and appreciated as the exhibitions of the National Academy.*"

As the Professor's reminiscences suggest, he had more than a passing interest in the contemporary equivalent of pop art—indeed, his place was "a museum as well as a bar," to quote *Appleton's*, containing "all, or nearly all, the caricatures of celebrities, painted by Nast for the *bal d'opera* a few years ago; to these a good many additions have been made, so that Jerry Thomas's comic gallery is as well visited and appreciated as the exhibitions of the National

Academy." And well it might be—the walls of his saloon displayed caricatures of all the political and theatrical figures of the day, drawn by the most popular artists. Nast, though, was the star; the most celebrated and controversial caricaturist of his day, through his platform in *Harper's* magazine he was a political and cultural force to be reckoned with. When he did your caricature, you'd best make sure you saw it, and many of his subjects—e.g., Ulysses S. Grant—did just that.

It couldn't have hurt Thomas's collecting that he was an artist himself. When the writer Mr. Hingston encountered him at the Occidental, he noted that Thomas "is clever also with his pencil . . . and behind his bar are specimens of his skill as a draughtsman." Indeed, according to Thomas his work "Jerry Thomas's 'Original Dream,' which is a vision of all the famous men and women of America sitting together in three tiers . . . tickled P. T. Barnum so much that he came to ask me to make him one like it, only having him, of course, asleep in the big, crimson-cushioned, central arm-chair, instead of me." It's one of my fondest hopes that . . . some talented researcher in American art . . . track down one or both of these *Dreams*—and, while he or she is at it, the series of pictures where Nast, according to a contemporary newspaper, "delineated that head-barkeeper [i.e., Thomas] in nine tippling postures colossally."

In 1872, faced with the kind of massive rent increases that are an eternal characteristic of the New York real estate market, the Thomas brothers moved their operations uptown to 1239 Broadway, near West Thirtieth Street. That was in the heart of the rip-roaring Tenderloin, where New York came to unwind (either within the bounds of the law or without). Apparently it was business as usual. Thomas was surrounded by his pictures, and the place was, as one history of the

New York stage notes, "popular with Wall Street men and members of the theatrical profession"—key constituencies for building a clientele. Finance and celebrities.

In fact, Thomas's bar was popular enough to become proverbial, the name you would reach for when you were looking for an example of a New York saloon. It appears as such, anyway, in two of the popular dialect humor books by "Eli Perkins" (alias New York journalist Melville D. Landon), and in 1875, it even made it into poetry, when George Augustus Baker, Jr., included a stanza in his "Les Enfants Perdus," a bittersweet ode to New York's gilded youth, wherein the "juvenile Comuses" all drink champagne and are "known at Jerry Thomas's." But suddenly, thronged as his place was, Thomas was done, broke and had to sell his store to John Morrissey. That was in 1876, when he was pulling in at least $200 a day, at a time when a bar could turn a profit on $50 a week. (Alas, not even his artistic skills would help him; the patent he was awarded on February 1, 1876, for a kind of signboard "intended to represent a book suspended by the head-band or upper end as is very commonly done with directories or other books for public reference" failed to pull him out of the hole.) His obituaries blamed the closing on financial problems caused by buying stocks on margin. Knowing the Professor's clientele, and knowing his sporting proclivities, I have little reason to doubt them. Thus ended Jerry Thomas's run as a star.

With the closing of this, his last high-profile bar, Jerry Thomas was relegated to keeping establishments in out-of-the-way corners of the city, first at 3 Barclay Street, across the street from the faded glory that was the old Astor House hotel, and then—after a last Hail-Mary fling at easy money in Denver and Leadville, where gold fever was again running high—on Sixth Avenue and West Tenth Street, under the

Elevated tracks across from the Jefferson Market Police Court. In both of these, apparently, he was without his brother, George, who wisely retired from the saloon trade sometime around then and went into banking, although he still appeared as a member of Thomas's enigmatic Gourd Club.

In March 1882, the Professor had to sell out for good. This time the pictures had to go, too—auctioned off to various fellow-bartenders and Sarony, the famous portrait photographer. The highest price paid at his auction was a paltry $25, for a caricature of the editor of one of New York's second-tier newspapers. All the Hogarths together brought a mere $49.50.

From FOREST *to* FLASK

WILLIAM M. DOWD

While master distillers jealously guard the precise formulae for their whiskies, there is one bit of knowledge they readily share with one and all, competitor and consumer: Fine wood is the key to fine whiskey. Be it the first interaction between the charred interiors of new American oak or French Limousin oak casks and the new-make spirits or the ongoing chemical reactions of used barrels with the Canadian blends, the Scotch single malts, the Irish spirits, the casks create the colors, the subtle nuances of taste and aroma. The wood is a worldwide connector for all forms of spirits. To that end, I traced that most universally popular of all aging woods, the American white oak, from the Ozark Mountains forests of Arkansas to a huge cooperage in Louisville, Kentucky, as it was prepared to receive its first taste of spirits.

In most of life's undertakings, patience is a virtue. In whisky making, it is a requirement. And, in this era of worldwide efforts to improve the sustainability of the environment, it is becoming an absolute necessity.

It was a gray day as we stood on the Victors Point ridge high above a gentle curve in the Mississippi River not far from the

boyhood Missouri home of the legendary American writer and critic Mark Twain. Dr. Bill Lumsden picked up an acorn, held it between two fingers and observed to me, "Just think, in a hundred years or so this could be part of Glenmorangie whisky."

Now, *that* is long-range thinking. It also is part of The Glenmorangie Company's corporate mantra: sustainability of the forests, a zero-waste production stream, and a continued excellence of product.

We were in the mostly rural state of Missouri—far from its two true population centers of St. Louis and Kansas City, there to more fully understand the yin and yang of whisky and charred wood.

The trek itself offered a study in small-town Americana surrounded by heavy oak-growth woods in the Ozark Mountains. There, the Scottish distiller Glenmorangie works with the Missouri Conservation Department as well as with private commercial loggers to select white oak trees for the barrels that eventually will hold its new whiskies—after, of course, they have been seasoned by helping American bourbon mature for four to eight years.

The wood cannot be discounted in the whisky-making process, no matter whether it is Scotch, American, Irish, Canadian, or anything else. Most in the industry concur that aging in wood accounts for perhaps 60 percent of the taste of the finished product and, of course, for all of the beautiful hues of gold, amber, and copper that result from the chemical interaction of spirit and wood.

"I've experimented with putting new-make whisky into various woods," said Lumsden. "You never know when something pleasing will come out of it."

Lumsden had the opportunity in the mid- to late-1990s to try swamp, burr, chinkapin, and post oaks in prototype barrels that had been air-dried for eighteen months.

"'There's a high degree of spiciness in the swamp oak, and the burr oak has a pleasant oiliness, almost buttery.'"

"There's a high degree of spiciness in the swamp oak, and the burr oak has a pleasant oiliness, almost buttery. The others didn't provide much difference from American white oak."

Most people refer to Lumsden as the master distiller for the highland distillery located in Tain, Ross-shire, Scotland, but several years ago his title was broadened to "head of distilling and whisky creation." That's a fancy way of saying he *is* Morangie whisky.

Any complaints from traditionalists about his experimentations?

"Oh, some, but I put it down to jealousy," Lumsden said with a twinkle.

While the vast bulk of wood used for aging Glenmorangie whiskies is American white oak, German Black Forest oak also is used. With perhaps ninety different types of oaks in the world, plus the fact that numerous distillers also employ second-use sherry oak casks such as

Oloroso for aging some products, wood can be Lumsden's playground for a long time to come.

The process for taking wood from the forests to the whisky aging warehouses is as straightforward as it has been for centuries: Select the right tree, cut and shape it into the proper dimensions for barrels, assemble the casks, toast or char them, seal them against leakage, and send them on their way.

What has changed tremendously, however, is the quality and precision of each step in a world that only in recent decades has become attuned to the necessity for preserving natural resources.

Kristen Goodrich is a resource forester with the State of Missouri. She supervises, among other tracts, the Edward Anderson Conservation Area outside the little town of Hannibal where Twain created his immortal characters of Tom Sawyer and Huckleberry Finn.

"We have to manage the forests, or they'll die out in wide patches," she explained to me. "That's why we cut on maybe a fifteen-year cycle, during which we can track growth of various trees, thin out the stands of wood where we need to so the proper amount of sunlight can get through to the stronger trees, and so we can prevent disease. Luckily, this area is fairly pest- and disease-free."

The foresters attempt to encourage slow growth in trees, which results in fewer large holes in the wood and thus stronger, less porous wood for barrels. In addition, slow growth oak has more vanillins and oak lactones that help flavor the whiskies, and white oak contains a substance called tyloses that naturally blocks the sap-conducting pores of the wood.

Nutrient-poor soil is an inherent growth inhibitor, but the amount of competition among trees for growing space, water, and sunlight is managed by selective cutting and trimming. Once the trees are felled, they're shipped off to sawmills, such as a large facility in nearby Novelty, Missouri, one of three mills owned by the Cardwell Lumber Company and located about twenty miles from nowhere in particular.

It's a state-of-the-art complex, opened in December 2007. Leroy Cardwell, founder and owner of the mills, explains it this way:

"The saying is that you have to build three houses before you really get it right. Well, this mill is our third one, and I think we absolutely got it right."

Much of the automated equipment was designed and built on the grounds by Cardwell's son, Mark, an obviously gifted craftsman. Sawing, trimming, pressure fitting . . . virtually everything is guided by computers, although a sizable workforce continues to be needed to coax and prod and direct the wood through the maze of steps, a good thing in an area with few opportunities for employment.

Some of the less mechanical steps are done by a group of Amish workers. Those men, distinguished by the plain clothes, straw hats, and beards emblematic of their sect of what generally is known in the U.S. as Pennsylvania Dutch, are among the best workers because of their closed society's widely praised work ethic.

Nevertheless, the smoothness of the operation is guided by the custom-built machinery.

"Mark crafted everything in that building up there," said Bob Russell, pointing to an unprepossessing metal structure on the edge of the sawmill yard. "They hauled the pieces down here to the main mill and everything fit perfectly."

Russell is manager of mill operations for the Brown–Forman Cooperage, the largest barrel-making facility of its kind in the world. The sixty-three-year-old Louisville, Kentucky, company works with

Moet-Hennessy's Glenmorangie to meet barrel specifications. Russell is a walking encyclopedia of wood-cutting techniques and wood waste management processes.

"One of the things that has saved a large percentage of wood is the thinner, sharper saw bands that have been installed here at Cardwell," he explained. "With a narrower cut, there is less sawdust and fewer splinters, and consequently fewer pieces of wood wasted.

"Actually, in the final count there is zero waste overall because even scraps, splinters, chips, and sawdust have other uses, such as for fuel, animal bedding, and other products."

At the mill, logs are cut into manageable lengths, stripped of bark to reduce the amount of blade-dulling dirt and pebbles, cut in half and then in half again in what is known as a quarter-sawing technique

The charring of barrels

rather than flat sawing. It exposes the grain in the proper direction to promote good leaching during whisky aging. Those pieces then are run through devices that shape them into barrel-length staves for the fifty-gallon casks.

Some shorter scrap becomes "headers," the name used for both the tops and bottoms of the barrels. They are planed to create tongue-in-groove edges, pressure-squeezed into squares, then cut into circular shapes with the guidance of a laser-light circle.

Then it was on to the Brown-Forman Cooperage—formerly the Blue Grass Cooperage—where a half-million barrels are turned out each year. It is where the actual barrel shape comes into existence, with an assembly line of younger workers arranging rings of thirty-two staves with such grace and economy of movement the process appears almost dance-like.

" "It pays better than a lot of other jobs, but it's physically difficult, and after six or eight years, you often move on to other stations." "

"This is a job for young men," explained a supervisor. "It pays better than a lot of other jobs, but it's physically difficult, and after six or eight years, you often move on to other stations."

Indeed, as we moved through the process, it was apparent that the less physically wearing tasks were handled by older workers—things like moving barrels on and off conveyers, driving forklifts, stacking headers that have been coated with beeswax then run through a charring flame.

The charring of the barrels in huge gas-fired ovens is a mesmerizing sight. Rows of open-ended barrels are shuttled through the chambers on steel conveyer belts, pausing long enough for roaring tongues of flame to leap through them in controlled bursts that impart the charred interior that will release the characteristics of the wood into the aging whiskies.

As the barrels come out of the oven, the pop and hiss of burning wood can be heard, showers of tiny sparks quickly cooling as the ambient temperature of the factory floor counteracts the 500°F (260°C) atmosphere the barrels had just left.

Just as the wood that went into making the barrels has had its provenance coded, stamped and logged, each barrel receives a serial number and can be tracked for its entire useful life.

So, in the final analysis, is all this maneuvering really worth the effort?

To quote the aforementioned Mr. Twain, "Too much of anything is bad, but too much good whiskey is barely enough."

A WHISKEY FUELED SOUTHERN LEGEND

TOM WOLFE

*The author Tom Wolfe made a major stride toward
becoming an American literary star when he was just 34
by writing about another type of icon: a hard-charging
Southern stock-car champion and moonshine runner about
his own age. Wolfe's essay for the March 1965 issue
of* Esquire *magazine was called "The Last American
Hero Is Junior Johnson. Yes!" In this excerpt from that
work, which the magazine includes among its "greatest*
Esquire *stories ever published," we are treated to a look
at a defining personality and time that helped create the
mystique of American whiskey.*

Ten o'clock Sunday morning in the hills of North
Carolina. Cars, miles of cars, in every direction and that
old mothering North Carolina sun keeps exploding off
the windshields. Seventeen thousand people, me included, all of
us driving out Route 421, out to the stock car races at the North
Wilkesboro Speedway, 17,000 going out to a five-eighths-mile
track with a Coca-Cola sign out front. This is not to say there is
no preaching and shouting in the South this morning. There is
preaching and shouting. Any of us can turn on the old automobile
transistor radio and get all we want:

"They are greedy dogs. Yeah! They ride around in big cars. Unnh-hunh! And chase women. Yeah! And drink liquor. Unnh-hunh! And smoke cigars. Oh yes! And they are greedy dogs. Yeah! Unnh-hunh! Oh yes! Amen!"

Miles and miles of eye-busting pastel cars on the expressway, which roar right up into the hills, going to the stock-car races. In 10 years baseball—and the State of North Carolina alone used to have 44 professional baseball teams—is all over with in the South. We are all in the middle of a wild new thing, the Southern car world, and heading down the road on my way to see a breed such as sports never saw before—Southern stock-car drivers, all lined up in these two-ton mothers that go over 175 mph: Fireball Roberts, Freddie Lorenzen, Ned Jarrett, Richard Petty, and—the hardest of all the hard chargers, one of the fastest automobile racing drivers in history—yes! Junior Johnson.

"We are all in the middle of a wild new thing, the Southern car world . . ."

In this legend, here is a country boy, Junior Johnson, who learns to drive by running whiskey for his father, Johnson, Senior, one of the biggest copper still operators of all times, up in Ingle Hollow, near North Wilkesboro, in northwestern North Carolina, and grows up to be a famous stock-car racing driver, rich, grossing $100,000 in 1963, for example, respected, solid, idolized in his hometown and throughout the rural South, for that matter. There is all this about how good old boys would wake up in the middle of the night in the apple shacks and hear an overcharged engine roaring over Brushy Mountain and say, "Listen at him—there he goes!"

It was Junior Johnson specifically, however, who was famous for the "bootleg turn" or "about-face" in which, if the Alcohol Tax agents had a roadblock up for you or were too close behind, you threw the car into second gear, cocked the wheel, stepped on the accelerator and made the car's rear end skid around in a complete 180-degree arc, a complete about-face, and tore on back up the road exactly the way you came from. God! The Alcohol Tax agents used to burn over Junior Johnson.

"All the other drivers, the drivers driving Fords, Mercurys, Plymouths, Dodges, had literally millions when it is all added up in backing from the Ford and Chrysler corporations. Junior Johnson took them all on in a Chevrolet without one cent of backing from Detroit."

The Junior Johnson the [good old boys] like to remember is the Junior Johnson of 1963, who took on the whole field of NASCAR (National Association for Stock Car Auto Racing) Grand National racing with a Chevrolet. All the other drivers, the drivers driving Fords, Mercurys, Plymouths, Dodges, had literally millions when it is all added up in backing from the Ford and Chrysler corporations. Junior Johnson took them all on in a Chevrolet without one cent of backing from Detroit. Yet every race it was the same. It was never a question of whether anybody was going to *outrun* Junior Johnson. It was just a question of whether he was going to win or his car was going to break down, since, for one thing, half the time he had to make his own racing parts. And then the good old boys get to talking about whatever happened to that Chevrolet of Junior's, and the cabdriver says he knows. He says Junior Johnson is using that car to run liquor out of Wilkes County.

What does he mean? For Junior Johnson ever to go near another load of bootleg whiskey again, he would have to be insane. He has this huge racing income. He has two other businesses, a whole automated chicken farm with 42,000 chickens, a road-grading business—but the cabdriver says he has this dream Junior is still roaring down from Wilkes County. Junior Johnson has followers who need to keep him, symbolically, riding through nighttime like a demon. Madness! But Junior Johnson is one of the last of those sports stars who is not just an ace at the game itself, but a hero a whole people or class of people can identify with.

I had driven from the Greensboro Airport up to Wilkes County to see Junior Johnson on the occasion of one of the two yearly NASCAR Grand National stock-car races at the North Wilkesboro Speedway. Practically all the drivers are out there with their cars and their crews, a lot of guys in white coveralls. Then, finally, here comes Junior Johnson. How he does come on. He comes tooling across the infield in a big white dreamboat, a brand-new white Pontiac Catalina four-door hard-top sedan. He pulls up and as he gets out he seems to get more and more huge. First his crew-cut head and then a big jaw and then a bigger neck and then a huge torso, like a wrestler's, all done up rather modish and California modern, with a red-and-white candy-striped sport shirt, white ducks and loafers.

"How you doing?" says Junior Johnson, shaking hands, and then he says, "Hot enough for ye'uns?"

"Ye'uns," "we'uns," "h'it" for "it," "growed" for "grew," and a lot of other unusual past participles—Junior uses certain older forms of English, not exactly "Elizabethan," as they are sometimes called, but older forms of English preserved up-country in his territory, Ingle Hollow.

Junior is in an amiable mood. Like most up-hollow people, it turns out, Junior is reserved. His face seldom shows an emotion. He has three basic looks: amiable, amiable and a little shy, and dead serious.

Junior was a sensation in dirt track racing right from the start. Instead of going into the curves and just sliding and holding on for dear life like the other drivers, Junior developed the technique of throwing himself into a slide about 75 feet before the curve by cocking the wheel to the left slightly and gunning it, using the slide, not the brake, to slow down, so that he could pick up speed again halfway through the curve and come out of it like a shot. This was known as his "power slide," and every good old boy in North Carolina started saying Junior Johnson had learned that stunt doing those goddamned *about-faces* running away from the Alcohol Tax agents.

The next morning [at his family's house] Junior motions his hand out toward the hills and says, "I'd say nearly everybody in a 50-mile radius of here was in the whiskey business at one time or another. When we growed up here, everybody seemed to be more or less messing with whiskey, and myself and my two brothers did quite a bit of transporting. H'it was just a business, like any other business, far as we was concerned. H'it was a matter of survival. During the Depression here, people either had to do that or starve to death. H'it wasn't no gangster type of business or nothing. They's nobody that ever messed with it here that was ever out to hurt anybody. Even if they got caught, they never tried to shoot anybody or anything like that. Getting caught and pulling time, that was just part of it. H'it was just a business, like any other business."

The mountain-still operators had been running white liquor with hopped-up automobiles all during the Thirties. But it was during the war that the business was so hot out of Wilkes County, down to Charlotte, High Point, Greensboro, Winston-Salem, Salisbury, places like that; a night's run, by one car, would bring anywhere from $500 to $1,000. People had money all of a sudden. One car could carry twenty-two to twenty-five cases of white liquor. There were 12 half-gallon fruit jars full per case, so each load would have 132 gallons or more. It would sell to the distributor in the city for about $10 a gallon, when the market was good, of which the driver would get $2, as much as $300 for the night's work.

> *"'H'it was just a business, like any other business, far as we was concerned. H'it was a matter of survival.'"*

Junior and his older brothers, L.P. and Fred, worked that way with their father, Robert Glenn Johnson Sr., one of the biggest individual copper-still operators in the area. The fourth time he was arrested, the agents found a small fortune in working corn mash bubbling in the vats.

"My Daddy was always a hard worker," Junior is telling me. "He always wanted something a little bit better. A lot of people resented that and held that against him, but what he got, he always got h'it by hard work. There ain't no harder work in the world than making whiskey.

I don't know of any other business that compels you to get up at all times of night and go outdoors in the snow and everything else and work. H'it's the hardest way in the world to make a living, and I don't think anybody'd do it unless they had to."

Working mash wouldn't wait for a man. It started coming to a head when it got ready to and a man had to be there to take it off, out there in the woods, in the brush, in the brambles, in the muck, in the snow. There wasn't anything ever written down. Everything was cash on the spot. Different drivers liked to make the run at different times, but Junior and his brothers always liked to start out from 3 to 4 a.m. But it got so no matter when you started out you didn't have those roads to yourself.

> *"I don't know of any other business that compels you to get up at all times of night and go outdoors in the snow and everything else and work.'"*

"Some guys liked one time and some guys liked another time," Junior is saying, "but starting about midnight they'd be coming out of the woods from every direction. Some nights the whole road was full of bootleggers. It got so some nights they'd be somebody following you going just as fast as you were and you didn't know who h'it was, the law or somebody else hauling whiskey."

In those wild-ass times, with the money flush and good old boys from all over the county running that white liquor down the road 90 miles an hour and more than that if you try to crowd them a little bit—well, the funny thing was, it got to be competitive in an almost aesthetic, a pure sporting way. The way the good old boys got to hopping up their automobiles—it got to be a science practically. Everybody was looking to build a car faster than anybody ever had before. They practically got into industrial espionage over it.

And all over the rural South, hell, all over the South, the legends of wild-driving whiskey running got started. And it wasn't just the plain excitement of it. It was something deeper, the symbolism. It brought into a modern focus the whole business, one and a half centuries old, of the country people's rebellion against the Federals, against the seaboard establishment, their independence, their defiance of the outside world. And it was like a mythology for that and for something else that was happening, the whole wild thing of the car as the symbol of liberation in the postwar South.

Whiskey running certainly had a crazy game-like quality about it, considering that a boy might be sent up for two years or more if he were caught transporting. But these boys were just wild enough for that. There got to be a code about the chase. In Wilkes County nobody, neither the good old boys nor the agents, ever did anything that was going to hurt the other side physically. There was supposed to be some parts of the South where the boys used smoke screens and tack buckets. They had attachments in the rear of the cars, and if the agents got too close they would let loose a smoke screen to blind them or a slew of tacks to make them blow a tire. But nobody in Wilkes County ever did that because that was a good way for somebody to get killed. The good old boys knew back roads, dirt roads, up people's back lanes and every which way, and an agent would have to live in the North Carolina hills a lifetime to get to know them. Then one day in 1955 some agents snuck over the ridges and caught Junior Johnson at his daddy's still. Junior Johnson, the man couldn't *any*body catch!

The arrest caught Junior just as he was ready to really take off in his career as a stock-car driver. Junior says he hadn't been in the whiskey business in any shape or form, hadn't run a load of whiskey for two or three years, when he was arrested. He was sentenced to two years in the Federal reformatory in Chillicothe, Ohio.

"If the law felt I should have gone to jail, that's fine and dandy," Junior tells me. "But I don't think the true facts of the case justified the sentence I got. I never had been arrested in my life. I think they was punishing me for the past. People get a kick out of it because the officers can't catch somebody, and this angers them. Soon as I started getting publicity for racing, they started making it real hot for my family. I was out of the whiskey business, and they knew that, but they was just waiting to catch me on something. I got out after serving 10 months and three days of the sentence, but h'it was two or three years I was set back, about half of '56 and every bit of '57. H'it takes a year to really get back into h'it after something like that. I think I lost the prime of my racing career."

MEET DEWAR'S GUARDIAN LADY

CAROLINE DEWAR

Whisky is a man's game when it comes to making the final pronouncements, no matter the country of its origin. Not so at the iconic Dewar's complex where a woman reigns supreme. Stephanie McLeod, a tall, handsome woman whose path to the pinnacle of whisky creation was a winding one. In this essay, writer Caroline Dewar—no coincidence there—introduces us to McLeod and what goes into the job of being a master blender for a globally known brand. (Originally published in Whisky Magazine, *issue 79, Norfolk, England.)*

The master blender at Dewar's in Glasgow is a calm and collected presence as she welcomes you to the premises. Following Tom Aitken's retirement in summer 2006, Stephanie McLeod became one of only a small number of senior women on the production side of Scotch whisky.

Her role is quality and consistency guardian of the Dewar's blends and malts and of all incoming whiskies and casks. She will also be creator of any new offerings. Only in her 30s, she has put in plenty of hard work to get here, and it is a job she obviously enjoys.

So how did it happen? First there was a degree in food science from Strathclyde University. That was followed up by a stint at Barr's, the soft drink producer, and then four years as a research assistant on whisky back at Strathclyde. Part of her work there was sensory and chemical analysis which continues to inform her domain at Dewar's. "Part of my research was to unlock the secrets of maturation—and we've still not done it."

After that, a move to Wm. Lawson's QC team, which subsequently became part of Dewar's. In 2000 she was put in charge of the laboratory where she set up a sensory panel, a new feature there. In 2002 she was asked if she was interested in training formally as a blender and worked with Tom to deepen her expertise and knowledge.

""Part of my research was to unlock the secrets of maturation— and we've still not done it.""

So what are the day-to-day tasks of a master blender? Are they locked away in labs all day, creating? For Stephanie, her days involve running the two test laboratories apart from her own nosing lab, and those cover all ingredients from barley to bottle. Distillery samples undergo chemical and sensory analysis at each stage to check consistency.

Samples of new spirit, blend batches and production line samples are nosed. Reports are done for distilleries on whiskies received and e-mails and letters replied to. Casks are nosed to guard against mold or mustiness and to ensure they have the properties sought.

She supervises laboratory staff who look, among other things, at major volatile congeners in whisky. Copper content in new spirit is monitored—it is important as a catalyst in maturation but levels must not be too high.

"Is the female nose better?" Stephanie's view is that everyone has some ability in this area but some are better than others to start with, whether male or female. Practice and training help to develop a keener nose.

Enthusiasm is just as important to her.

Turning to the Dewar's blends and malts, how does Stephanie view the development of premium blends?

"This is of great interest to us," she says. "We have very buoyant forecasts for Asia. It's a very exciting time. Consumers now take more interest in flavor. Our premium blends are still growing in emerging markets. Dewar's 18 Years Old and Signature have been launched in the last three years, and our Dewar's 15 Years Old blended malt is currently in Taiwan only.

"'We're looking at our other malts to see what we might want to develop in line with what markets want too.'"

"Looking at our malt portfolio, Aberfeldy at 12 and 21 Years Old have only recently been formally launched in the U.S. We're looking at our other malts to see what we might want to develop in line with what markets want too. They are currently available only at the distilleries and at Dewar's World of Whisky."

Those who have never encountered a blender might be curious as to how they go about that task. How does Stephanie begin blend creation, and can a move from small test to large volume change the liquid?

"The brief is always based on general flavor and specific age profiles. I start by thinking about the flavor profile to be created.

"Usually, I think of the blend as a structure. I begin with my framework malts and then the malts I want to hang on there that will add interest and complexity. Various permutations of the malt blend are sensory analyzed (nose, taste, mouthfeel, color), always blind, and a selection is made. For the grain element—again, test blends are compiled and then blended with the malt element. A number of blends are made up, analyzed blind and preferences selected.

"These are then presented to a trained sensory team, blind, over several days, and a preferred blend emerges," she goes on. "I work with very small volumes to begin with, but generally I've found that the parity between the small test volume—one liter or so—and the actual blend to be excellent, so far."

What about finishes? Stephanie says: "We haven't gone down that route in Dewar's yet. They seem to be doing well. It certainly gives more choice and variety but is not something I would buy myself."

In terms of blends she places no particular one on a pedestal but simply states that Dewar's own blends are very precious to her. Her main ambition is to build on the work of previous blenders. She wants the best wood and the best new-make spirit.

"If a market would like a new blend, it's my job to produce it in terms of flavor profile required. I would like to create something of my own—I'm a scientist, I love experimenting! But only when I have time. As a group, Bacardi is very interested in innovation and actively encourages it, within reason."

I asked Stephanie if, like some old-school blenders, she throws a fit if anyone comes into the labs wearing perfume or aftershave.

"No, but I don't like it. You know, it's a big sacrifice that I can't wear perfume every day. I just prefer to encourage people on our sensory panels not to wear anything like that."

Not irascible then, which is the impression you get from the start with Stephanie. Calm assurance prevails.

The
MICRO-DISTILLING MOVEMENT

DAVID PORT

The whiskey giants are secure in their place in the world of commercial spirits, but a growing number of artisans—some of whom began as hobbyists or winemakers—are chipping away at them by offering the consumer many more choices of small-batch whiskies. In some states—New York, for example—the phenomenon has gained such strength that statewide craft distillers associations have been formed to help lobby and market the products. In this essay originally written for **Entrepreneur** *magazine, journalist David Port takes a broad look at the modern movement.*

W e're making absinthe today," says Scott Leopold with a hint of mischief in his voice. That explains the pungent aroma of anise wafting into his office from his small but apparently thriving liquor distilling operation.

His brother and business partner, master distiller Todd Leopold, is in the back concocting a fresh batch of the cloudy, 130-proof spirit. Until recently, absinthe was illegal to produce in the United States because it was (erroneously) believed to contain hallucinogenic ingredients.

Today, the Leopold Bros.' micro-distillery, located in a nondescript industrial complex on the outskirts of Denver, Colorado, makes absinthe that will eventually sell for about $70 a bottle. Tomorrow it could be one of several liqueurs—or perhaps a gin, vodka or whisky, or even a test batch of the new Pisco or triple sec—the brothers plan to introduce.

Founded in Michigan as a brewpub and now exclusively a distillery, Leopold Bros. is part of a growing micro-distillery movement in the United States. The number of small-batch distilleries has more than doubled in just a few years, from fewer than 80 in 2006 to 165 in 2009, says Bill Owens, founder of the American Distilling Institute.

Boutique, artisan, craft, small-batch, micro—whatever the moniker, these independent, entrepreneurial distillers are fueling a "renaissance in American spirit-making," Owens says.

Not only are entrepreneurs building viable, sustainable businesses using traditional, hands-on distilling techniques, they are enthusiastically embracing the distinctly American "moonshine culture," he says. "I think there's something very, very deep in the culture where, if you control the process of making something that alters consciousness, you control a kind of magic. There's allure in that."

Carrying the mystical mantle of the moonshine culture is all the more alluring if you make a profit doing so. Using what Scott

Leopold describes as an "ultra-low-overhead" business model—no retail storefront or distillery tours, a handful of employees, strictly grassroots marketing with virtually no advertising—the Leopold Bros. distilling operations was cash-flow-positive after 18 months.

Fellow Denver micro-distiller Stranahan's, maker of Stranahan's Colorado Whisky, became profitable in its fifth year. Like Leopold Bros., which recently invested $100,000 in a new still to increase production capacity, Stranahan's is in growth mode, founder Jess Graber says. In 2009, the company purchased and moved into its own facility, in the process adding new equipment to triple its whisky-making capacity. Stranahan's Colorado Whisky, which tastes like a hybrid of scotch and bourbon, is available in 36 states and a handful of countries outside the U.S.

Stranahan's has succeeded "beyond my wildest dreams," gushes Graber, a former contractor and volunteer fireman who admittedly has been "experimenting" with distilling techniques since the early 1970s. Graber says he's savoring his success in the micro-distilling business and the lifestyle that comes with it.

"It's crazy and it's fun, and it's almost like I'm beyond the worrying stage now," Graber says.

Stranahan's is at the forefront of a micro-distillery movement that reminds some observers of the microbrewery uprising that in the 1980s and '90s enlivened the domestic beer market with entrepreneurial spirit, not to mention better-tasting suds.

"The climate is certainly similar," says Brett Pontoni, the specialty spirits buyer at Binny's Beverage Depot, a huge Chicago-based liquor retailer and acknowledged cheerleader for the micro-distillery movement. "There's a perception that a lot of the big guys"— corporate distillers—"are not fulfilling a need for quality, so you have entrepreneurs trying to fill the gaps the big guys aren't hitting."

Similarities aside, to say the micro-distillery movement will ever match the scope of the microbrewery craze would be an overstatement, Pontoni and Owens agree.

"We might get to 400 [craft distillers in the U.S.]," Owens says, "but we're not going to get to 1,500, like the microbreweries have."

""They're not bringing people in off the sidelines. What they are doing is getting consumers with taste to try their products.""

Unlike the microbrewery movement, which attracted new beer drinkers, "I don't think micro-distillers are creating new consumers of distilled spirits," Pontoni says. "They're not bringing people in off the sidelines. What they are doing is getting consumers with taste to try their products."

Another difference between the first wave of microbrewers and the micro-distillers of today is business acumen, Pontoni observes. Micro-distillers in general appear to have a sounder approach to capitalizing and scaling up their operations, he says.

Even with a solid business plan and a good product, "It's a definite challenge" wresting market share from huge corporate distillers, which represent the chief competition, says Chris Sule. Sule is master distiller at Celebration Distillation, which produces highly decorated, small-batch rums out of its facility in the Ninth Ward of New Orleans.

As with the spirits they produce, micro-distilleries have varying recipes for success. Celebration Distillation and Stranahan's have elected to stick to a single core product, while Leopold Bros. has found success by making a broad range of products.

Meanwhile, the strategy for some distillers is to market themselves as destinations, with conference centers, facility tours, restaurants, gift shops and the like to provide additional revenue streams. Others, like Leopold Bros., are sticking strictly to distilling without marketing themselves much at all.

With shrewd business tactics and products that stack up against the best the big distillers have to offer, infused with a hint of the moonshiner mind-set, micro-distillers are primed to compete over the long run, Graber says.

"We're fighting for shelf space just like the big guys. We don't make enough [spirits] to rob much market share from them but, trust me, the distilling establishment knows who we are."

A SPIRITS QUOTEBOOK

Long before and long after the Irish playwright Oscar Wilde reworded the aphorism "Drink is the curse of the working class" to the more amusing "Work is the curse of the drinking class," pithy quotes about spirits have been traded around the world. Sometimes they are slightly skewed in translation, stretched and reshaped a bit in the re-telling, or attributed to more than one originator. But, in the final analysis, they provide insights and amusements to society.

"Too much of anything is bad, but too much of good whiskey is barely enough."
–Author Mark Twain

✤

"For a bad hangover take the juice of two quarts of whisky."
– Jazz musician and bandleader Eddie Condon

✤

"I went on a diet, swore off drinking and heavy eating, and in fourteen days I lost two weeks."

–American nightclub comic Joe E. Lewis

✤

"There is no such thing as bad whiskey. Some whiskeys just happen to be better than others. But a man shouldn't fool with booze until he's 50; then he's a damn fool if he doesn't."

–Author William Faulkner

⚜

"Whiskey has killed more men than bullets, but most men would rather be full of whiskey than bullets."

–Writer Logan Pearsall Smith

⚜

"When it's 3rd-and-10, you can take the milk drinkers and I'll take the whiskey drinkers every time."

–Former Green Bay Packers football star
Max McGee

⚜

"I like whiskey. I always did, and that is why I never drink it."

–Confederate General Robert E. Lee

⚜

"I always carry a bottle of whiskey in case of snakebite. I also carry a small snake."

–Actor W. C. Fields

⚜

"The water was not fit to drink. To make it palatable, we had to add whisky. By diligent effort, I learnt to like it."

–Sir Winston Churchill

⚜

"They say some of my stars drink whiskey. But, I have found that the ones who drink milkshakes don't win many ball games."

–Hall of Fame baseball manager Casey Stengel

✤

"A respectable amount of bourbon to pour in a glass is about two fingers' worth. Lucky for me, I have big fingers."

–American distiller Frederick Booker Noe II

✤

"No married man is genuinely happy if he has to drink worse whiskey than he used to drink when he was single."

–American journalist H.L. Mencken

✤

"The light music of whiskey falling into a glass—an agreeable interlude."

–Irish novelist James Joyce

✤

"There were years when I was a beer and tequila guy, then I got real fat. And then I found that you could actually go on a diet and drink Scotch. Then I got hooked on Scotch, and if you get hooked on Scotch, then everything else just tastes wrong."

–Comedian Ron White

✤

"I love to sing, and I love to drink Scotch. Most people would rather hear me drink Scotch."

–Actor and monologist George Burns

✤

"*I like my whisky old and my women young.*"

–Australian film actor Errol Flynn

✤

"*Everyone who drinks is not a poet. Some of us drink because we're not poets.*"

–Actor Dudley Moore in the movie *Arthur*

✤

"*Champagne's funny stuff. I'm used to whiskey. Whiskey is a slap on the back, and champagne's a heavy mist before my eyes.*"

–Actor Jimmy Stewart in *The Philadelphia Story*

✤

"*I should never have switched from Scotch to martinis.*"

–Alleged last words of movie star
Humphrey Bogart

✤

"*I just had nineteen shots of whiskey. I think that's a record.*"

–Alleged last words of Welsh poet and writer
Dylan Thomas

✤

"*We borrowed golf from Scotland as we borrowed whiskey. Not because it is Scottish, but because it is good.*"

–Nineteenth-century golf expert
Horace G. Hutchinson

✤

"*I have drunk since I was 15, and few things have given me more pleasure. When you work hard all day with your head and know you must work again the next*" day, what else can change your ideas and make them run on a different plane like whiskey? When you are cold and wet what else can warm you?"

–Novelist Ernest Hemingway

✤

"I think a man ought to get drunk at least twice a year just on principle, so he won't let himself get snotty about it."

–Novelist Raymond Chandler

✤

"When I read about the evils of drinking, I gave up reading."

–Comedian Henny Youngman

✤

"The problem with the world is that everyone is a few drinks behind."

–Actor Humphrey Bogart

✤

"I think a guy who's had just the right amount of booze can sing the blues a hell of a lot better than a guy who is stone sober."

–Country singer Charlie Rich

✤

"Part of the $10 million I spent on gambling, part on booze, and part on women. The rest I spent foolishly."

–Actor George Raft

✤

"I drink to make other people more interesting."

–American critic and author George Jean Nathan

✤

"I am not a heavy drinker. I can sometimes go for hours without touching a drop."

–Playwright Noel Coward

⚓

"I feel sorry for people who don't drink. They wake up in the morning and that's the best they are going to feel all day."

–Singer-actor Frank Sinatra

⚓

"I have to think hard to name an interesting man who does not drink."

–Actor Richard Burton

⚓

"Candy is dandy, but liquor is quicker."

–American poet Ogden Nash

⚓

"We can make liquor to sweeten our lips, of pumpkins and parsnips and walnut-tree chips."

–Writer-philosopher Henry David Thoreau

⚓

"Prohibition is better than no liquor at all."

–American writer/actor/philosopher Will Rogers

⚓

GLOSSARY

An alphabetically arranged pocket guide to some terms frequently used in the spirits trade.

A

ABV—Abbreviation for alcohol by volume: i.e., the alcohol strength of a whiskey measured as a percentage part in relation to the liquid as a whole.

Absolute Alcohol—Ethyl alcohol containing 1 percent or less weight by water.

Age—The age of the youngest component of the whiskey.

Aging—The maturation of the whiskey in barrels.

Alcohol—Any fermented liquid that contains ethyl alcohol or ethanol (CH_3CH_2OH).

Alembic—An alchemical still consisting of two vessels connected by a tube.

Angels' Share—The amount of whiskey lost through evaporation during the aging process.

B

Balanced—A finished spirit with no one element dominating.

Barley Malt—The grain after it has soaked, had sprouts removed, been dried, and crushed to a powder.

Barrel—Wooden whiskey barrel holds 53 U.S. gallons or 44 Imperial gallons, or 200.6 liters.

Beer Barrel—A stainless steel barrel holding thirty-one gallons.

Batch Distillation—Occurs when the amount going into the still and the amount going out are not supposed to be the same all the time. Opposite of continuous distillation.

Blended Whiskey—A combination of straight whiskey and neutral grain spirits, usually with the straight whiskey at least 20 percent more in proportion. Sold at 80 proof.

Blended Malt Whiskey—A mix of single malt whiskies from different distilleries.

Bond—Maturing whiskey on which there is no excise tax yet paid.

Bottled in Bond—At least four years old, bottled at 100 proof (50 percent alcohol), and produced in one distilling, then sorted and bottled at a bonding warehouse under government supervision.

Bourbon—A spirit made, by U.S. federal regulations, from a grain mash of at least 51 percent corn, matured in new, charred American white oak barrels, and aged at least two years. Named for the Tennessee county in which it first was produced.

Brandy—A distilled wine. The name comes from the Dutch *brandewijn* (burnt wine), describing wine that had been boiled to distill it.

Bung—The cork or stopper used in a wooden barrel.

Butt—A 500-liter barrel.

C

Call Drink—Drink made with specified brands.

Canadian Whiskey—A blended product of a rye, corn, and malt mash that, by Canadian law, is aged in "small wood"—as opposed to large tanks—for at least three years; contains no less than 40 percent alcohol by volume (80 proof); may be flavored but no more than 9.09 percent, and then only by using certain substances, most of which are subject to their own aging requirements.

Cask—The barrel in which whiskey is matured.

Cask Strength—Whiskey bottled without being diluted.

Charring—Flame-burning the interior of a barrel to allow a chemical process that adds color and flavor to the aging whiskey by releasing vanillin and exposing the whiskey to tannins, lignin, and hemicellulose. It can be lightly toasted or heavily charred or something in between.

Chill Filtering—Chilling whiskey to filter it and allow removal of congeners. Done to prevent haze in the whiskey.

Coffey Still—Also known as a continuous or patent still, invented by Irishman Aeneas Coffey. It allows the continuous distillation of wash.

Congeners—Chemical compounds found in whiskey and created during fermentation, distillation, and maturation.

Continuous Distillation—Mash is continuously put into the still and product is drawn out at the same time. The amount going into the still and the amount leaving the still should always equal each other at any time. Opposite of batch distillation.

Cooperage—A barrel-making facility.

Cuts—The middle, or best, portion of the spirit coming off the spirit still.

D

Dextrose—Basic sugar, also called corn sugar. An optional base for making moonshine.

Distillation—The process of heating a liquid to boiling, thus turning the liquid into a gas that releases hot vapors that are caught and cooled so they return to a purer liquid form.

Distilled Beverage—A beverage, liquor, or spirit in drinkable form containing ethanol and produced by distilling fermented grain, fruit, or vegetables. Excludes beer and wine.

Distilled Spirits Council of the United States—DISCUS, as it is commonly known, is the lobbying and educational organization representing more distillers than any other organization.

E

Eau de Vie—French for "water of life." A colorless fruit brandy.

Estery—The chemical esters in the aroma, usually light and floral or fruity.

Ethanol—The most commonly used alcohol. It has been produced and consumed by humans for millennia, in the form of fermented and distilled alcoholic beverages. It also may be used as a fuel.

F

Feints—The impure spirit produced from the end of the second distillation. Also known as tails. They usually are re-distilled.

Fermentation—The process by which yeast interacts with the sugars in a juice or mash to release ethanol and carbon dioxide.

Finish—The residual feel of a spirit after it has been swallowed.

Fortification—The process of adding alcohol to increase its content percentage.

Fortified Wine—Wine to which a spirit has been added.

Fusel Oils— Also known as fusel alcohols, or potato oil in Europe. They are higher-order alcohols—those with more than two carbon atoms— formed by fermentation. Bitter tasting, usually found in tails.

G

Gooseneck Still—Technically a pot still, except for the tall, broad neck that allows separation to hold back most of the fusel oils from the distillate while retaining the desired flavors.

Grain Neutral Spirits—Alcohol distilled from grain at 190 proof. Nearly colorless and tasteless.

Grain Whiskey—Whiskies made from corn or wheat.

H

Headers—The circular tops and bottoms of spirits and wine barrels.

High Wines—The liquid contained in the second still during the distillation process.

Highball—A drink made of a spirit and carbonated water or soft drink in a tall glass with ice.

Hogshead—A 250-liter barrel.

I

Irish Whiskey—Made from a blend of barley malt whiskies and grain whiskies. The malt is dried in coal-fired kilns. Usually made at 86 proof, and made only in Ireland. Always triple distilled.

J

Jigger—A bartending tool used to measure liquor. Named for the unit of liquid it typically measures, a 1.5 fluid ounce (44 ml) jigger or shot. Capacity may vary depending on location.

Jug Yeast—Wild yeast, so called because it must be kept in a liquid medium and constantly tended to prevent being spoiled by an undesirable strain.

Jura—An island in Scotland's Inner Hebrides that has its own commercial distillery.

K

Kiln—A high-heat furnace sometimes used for drying barley.

L

Limousin—An area in central France that produces a much-prized form of oak, used in maturing wines and spirits.

Lincoln County Process—The practice of filtering corn whiskey through charcoal, thus changing the spirit from bourbon to Tennessee sipping whiskey. Named for the county where the practice began.

Liqueurs—A spirit infused with flavoring ingredients and sweeter than straight alcohol.

Low Wines—The result of the first distillation in the wash still. Has an alcohol content of about 20 percent.

M

Malt, Malted Grain—Barley soaked in water, then spread to dry in order to promote germination.

Marrying—Period in which whiskies mixed from different batches are allowed to combine and mature.

Mash—The mixture resulting from combining hot water and malted grain then steeping it at various temperatures to let enzymes in the malt break down the starch in the grain into sugars. After the starches in the grain have been enzymatically broken down into sugars, it is called the wort.

Mash Tun—The large tub or container holding hot water and grist for the mashing process.

Micro-Distillery—Small distillery, often run by one or two people, creating alcoholic beverages in small batches on a limited basis.

Moonshine—Refers to non-commercially distilled corn whiskey made in an unlicensed—hence, illegal—still. So-called because it often was/is made in secluded places by the light of the moon to avoid detection by law enforcement agencies. Other terms for it include "white lightning," "hooch," and "mountain dew."

N

Neat—A drink of straight liquor with no mixer.

Neutral Grain Spirit—Alcohol of 190 or higher proof. Used worldwide in the manufacture of vodka, gin, and whiskey.

New Make—Newly made, clear spirit. Usually less than three years old.

Nose—The aroma of the whiskey.

Nosing—The process of smelling, rather than tasting, the spirit to ascertain its olfactory properties.

O

Oloroso—A type of Spanish sherry (*oloroso* means "scented"). Former oloroso barrels are used to help mature some whiskies to add certain fragrance and taste elements.

On the Rocks—A drink poured over, or containing, ice.

P

Patent Still—Another name for the Coffey still.

Peat—The mucky decomposed plant matter found in turf bogs throughout Ireland and Scotland. It is primarily used as fuel. In traditional Scottish whisky making, it is the fuel for drying malted barley, thus imparting a smoky taste.

Pitch—The process of adding yeast to the wash.

Pot Still—A copper container in which distillation takes place.

Prohibition—A period in the United States (1920–1933) during which the manufacture, sale, and consumption of alcoholic beverages was illegal. Otherwise known as the Volstead Act, the power behind the Eighteenth Amendment to the U.S. Constitution that created Prohibition.

Proof—The measurement of the alcohol content of a spirit, expressed as a number double its alcohol by volume (ABV): i.e., 80 proof whiskey contains 40 percent alcohol in its final form.

Pure Pot Still Whiskey—A designation unique to some Irish whiskey. It refers to whiskey made from 100 percent barley, mixed malted and unmalted, and distilled in a pot still.

Q

Quaich—A shallow two-handled Scottish drinking cup or bowl. The name comes from the Scottish Gaelic word *cuach*, meaning "cup."

R

Rackhouse—The building in which whiskey is aged. Also known as a warehouse.

Reflux—When vapors condense and re-vaporize in the column of a still.

Run—Clear alcohol liquid produced by the distilling process.

S

Scotch—A grain spirit manufactured in Scotland under regulations of the Scotch Whisky Association.

Scotch Whisky Association—The official trade organization representing the majority of Scotland's whisky distillers.

Single Malt—A whiskey that is the product of an individual distillery rather than a mixture.

Small Batch—Proprietary whiskies made in limited quantities, usually as a higher-priced product.

Sour Mash Whiskey—A portion of old mash is mixed with new to help affect the character of the flavor.

Spirit Safe—A legally mandated device in which the stillman measures the alcohol strength, and determines when to switch to and from the "hearth" of the run.

Staves—The wooden slats that make up the main body of a barrel.

Still—An apparatus that allows a heated mixture to turn to steam then cool and condense into purer liquid. Mostly used to produce distilled beverages and ethyl alcohol.

T

Tail—Another word for feints.

Tennessee Whiskey—Similar to bourbon, except that it undergoes a filtration through charcoal, known as the Lincoln County Process.

Tipple—Refers to either a generic word for an alcoholic drink or the act of drinking one such.

Tub—A fifty-five-gallon stainless steel or plastic barrel used as a fermentation vessel.

U

Uisge beatha—Gaelic word, pronounced *wiz key bay tah*, meaning "water of life." The modern word whiskey comes from its first two syllables.

V

Vatted Whiskey—Also called pure malt. A blend of single malts from more than one distillery and with differing ages. Vatted malts contain only malt whiskies, no grain whiskies.

Vatting—Mixing similar whiskies from a single distillery, but from different casks.

Vodka—From the Russian word for "water" (*wodka* in Polish). A colorless, odorless, tasteless distillation from grain, potatoes, or other organic matter.

W

Wash—The fermented liquid before it is pumped into the wash still for the first distillation.

Well Drink—Drink made with unspecified brands. The "house brands" at a bar.

Wort—The mash after the starches in the grain have been broken down into sugars.

XYZ

X Waters—An old Irish term for whiskies.

Yeast—A living micro-organism that feeds on sugar to produce alcohol as one of its byproducts.

SOURCES

The text of "A Whiskey Fueled Southern Legend" originally appeared under the title "The Last American Hero Is Junior Johnson. Yes!" in the March 1965 issue of Esquire magazine. Excerpt from The Kandy-Colored Tangerine-Flake Streamline Baby reprinted by permission of SLL/Sterling Lord Literistic, Inc. Copyright by Thomas K. Wolfe, Jr.

The text of "The Mathematics of Prohibition" originally appeared under the title "The Hummingbird That Went to Mars" in Last Call: The Rise and Fall of Prohibition by Daniel Okrent. Reprinted with the permission of Scribner, a Division of Simon & Schuster, Inc. Copyright © 2010 by Last Laugh, Inc. All rights reserved.

The text of "The Inestimable Jerry Thomas" originally appeared in the first chapter (entitled "'Professor' Jerry Thomas: Jupiter Olympus of the Bar") of IMBIBE! by David Wondrich. Excerpt from IMBIBE! copyright © 2007 by David Wondrich. Used by permission of Perigree Books, an imprint of Penguin Group (USA) Inc.

The text of "From Rum to Whiskey in the New U.S.A." was originally published in Chapter 6 (entitled "The Drinks That Built America") of A History of the World in Six Glasses by Tom Standage (Walker Publishing Co., 2005). Reprinted with permission.

The text of "A Brief History of Distilling" was originally published in The Art of Distilling Whiskey and Other Sports, edited by Bill Owens and Alan Dikty (Quarry Books, 2009). Reprinted with permission.

The text of "The Ubiquitous Beams" was originally published in Bourbon, Straight: The Uncut and Unfiltered Story of American Whiskey by Charles K. Cowdery (Made and Bottled in Kentucky, 2004). Reprinted with permission.

The text of "The Man in the Overcoat" is excerpted from a passage in the oral history "Cumberland, Maryland, Through the Eyes of Herman J. Miller," compiled by Dr. Harry Stegmaier. Reprinted with permission.

The text of "Moonshine and the Morning Glass" is excerpted from a passage in Rumrunners and Revenuers: Prohibition in Vermont *by Scott Wheeler (New England Press Inc., 2002). Reprinted with permission.*

The text of "George Smith and the Glenlivet" is excerpted from passages in A Double Scotch: How Chivas Regal and the Glenlivet Became Global Icons *by F. Paul Pacult. Copyright © 2005 John Wiley & Sons, Inc. Reproduced with permission of John Wiley & Sons, Inc.*

The text of "Jack Daniel: A Small Man Becomes a Giant" is excerpted from passages in Blood & Whiskey: The Life and Times of Jack Daniel *by Peter Krass. Copyright © 2004 John Wiley & Sons, Inc. Reproduced with permission of John Wiley & Sons, Inc.*

The text of "A Wee Bit of Scotland in Japan" by Richard Hendy originally appeared on the blog www.spikejapan.wordpress.com. Reprinted with permission.

The text of "The Micro-Distilling Movement" by David Port originally appeared under the title "Make Room at the Bar," © 2009 by Entrepreneur Media, Inc. All rights reserved. Source: http://www.entrepreneur.com/article/202282 with permission of Entrepreneur Media, Inc.

The text of "The Irish Whiskey Titans" is excerpted from a passage in Irish Whiskey: A 1000 Year Tradition *by Malachy Magee, © 1998 The O'Brien Press Limited. Reprinted with permission.*

The text of "Grant, Babcock, and the Whiskey Ring" by Timothy Rives originally appeared in Prologue, *Fall 2000. Reprinted with permission.*

The text of "The Original Scotch and Its Heirs" is excerpted from a passage in Whiskeypedia: A Gazetteer of Scotch Whiskey *by Charles MacLean, © 2009 Birlinn Ltd. Reprinted with permission.*

"How to . . . Become a Collector" by Jennifer Harper originally appeared under the title "Collecting Whisky" in Scottish Field magazine. Reprinted with permission.

"From Forest to Flask: Wed In the Wood" by William M. Dowd was originally published in Whisky Magazine, issue #72. Reprinted with permission.

"Meet Dewar's Guardian Lady" by Caroline Dewar was originally published in Whisky Magazine, issue #79. Reprinted with permission.

"All the Rage in the Raj" by Tom Bruce-Gardyne was originally published in Whisky Magazine, issue #29. Reprinted with permission.

"The Case of Capone's Whiskey" by Jim Leggett was originally published in Whisky Magazine, issue #50. Reprinted with permission.

"How to . . . Taste Without 'Cups of Despair'" by Jim Murray was originally published in Whisky Magazine, issue #1. Reprinted with permission.

The text of "How to . . . Try Home Vatting" by Moritz Kallmeyer originally appeared under the title "The Living Cask: Re-discovering an Ancient Practice" on the website of Drayman's Brewery and Distillery, www.draymans.com. Reprinted with permission.

PICTURE CREDITS

We would like to acknowledge the following contributors who sent their bottle and label images.

Page 12 Old Rip Van Winkle Distillery; 13, top Lark Distillery, bottom Brown-Forman Corporation; 14, top Beam Global Spirits & Wine, Inc./Knob Creek Distillery Company, bottom Beam Global Spirits & Wine, Inc./Maker's Mark Distillery, Inc.; 15, SKYY Spirits LLC/Austin, Nichols Distilling Company; 17, The Welsh Whisky Company/Penderyn Distillery; 20, Bruichladdich Distillery; 21, Buffalo Trace Distillery; 30, Beam Global Spirits & Wine/Ardmore Distillery Company Limited; 49, Brown-Forman Corporation/Jack Daniel Distillery; 56, William Grant & Sons Irish Brands Ltd.; 63, DBC PR+New Media/Beam Global Spirits and Wine; 64, Beam Global Spirits and Wine/The Old Crow Distillery Company 66, DBC PR+New Media/Beam Global Spirits and Wine; 81, Heaven Hill Distilleries, Inc.; 105, Hunter Public Relations/John Walker & Sons; 107, Beam Global Spirits and Wine; 108, Brown-Forman Corporation; 128, The Edrington Group Ltd.; 134, Asahi Breweries, Ltd./The Nikka Whisky Distilling Co., Ltd.; 140, De Kock Communications (DKC)/ James Sedgwick Distillery; 173, The Glenmorangie Company; 194, Tuthilltown Spirits Distillers; 195, 5 Stone Advertising/Stranahan's Colorado Whiskey; 197, Brown-Forman Corporation/The Woodford Reserve Distillery.

INDEX

Alcohol
    etymology of, 3
    legal definition of whiskey, 8
    184 proof, 18–19
American Whiskey Trail, 5–6
    America, whiskey and
    Colonial Period, 76–82
    legalities and politics, 5–6, 7–8, 51–52.
        See also Bootleggers; Prohibition;
        Smuggling; Whiskey Ring
    present day, 19–20
    Whiskey Ring and, 83–95
Arabs and Persians, 2–3

Babcock, Gen. Orville E., 84–85, 86–87,
    90–95
Barnard, Alfred, 59, 72
Barrels, 68, 140, 172, 173–179
Beam family, 61–68
    about: overview of, 61–62
    Beauregard "Jim," 64, 65–67
    Booker Noe and, 66, 67–68
    business, plant, and brand development,
        61–68
    Charlie, 62
    David and sons, 63, 65
    Everett, 62, 65
    Guy, 62, 63–64
    Harry, 62, 65
    Joe, 62, 64–65, 66
    Johannes Jacob "Jake," 62–63
    Joseph B., 63
    Minor Case, 63
    Otis, 62, 65
    size of, 61
    Walter (Toddy), 64
Beck, James Montgomery, 117

Bell, Andrew, 151–152
Bell, C. S., 91
Ben Nevis distillery, 135
Blends
    about: overview of, 32
    Alfred Barnard on, 72
    awards, 132
    growth of, 32, 71–73
    master blender of Dewar's and, 189–192
    origin of, 71
    qualities of, 32, 71
    South African. *See* South Africa, whisky
        and
    vatted whiskey, 156–159
    whiskey names and, 11
Boers and Boer War, 145–146
Bootleggers. *See also* Prohibition
    Detroit, 107–108
    Junior Johnson and, 180–188
    Maryland/Pennsylvania, 98–100
Bow Street distillery, 55–57
Bradford, David, 80
Bristow, Benjamin H., 88–90, 91
Brown-Forman Cooperage, 176–177,
    178–179
Bruce-Gardyne, Thomas, 124
Bruichladdich Distillery, 18–19, 20, 21

Call, Dan, 47–48, 51, 52
Cardhu, 73
Cardwell Lumber Company, 176–177
Celebration Distillation, 197
Chivas Brothers, 21, 32
Collecting whiskies, 150–152
Colonial Period, 76–82
Colony, Myron, 89–90
Cowan, Jessie Roberta "Rita," 133–135